# Women of the Bible

## Heroines and the Lessons They Can Still Teach Us

AMERICAN BIBLE SOCIETY

## TIME HOME ENTERTAINMENT

**PUBLISHER** Jim Childs
**VICE PRESIDENT, BRAND & DIGITAL STRATEGY** Steven Sandonato
**EXECUTIVE DIRECTOR, MARKETING SERVICES** Carol Pittard
**EXECUTIVE DIRECTOR, RETAIL & SPECIAL SALES** Tom Mifsud
**EXECUTIVE PUBLISHING DIRECTOR** Joy Bomba
**DIRECTOR, BOOKAZINE DEVELOPMENT & MARKETING** Laura Adam
**VICE PRESIDENT, FINANCE** Vandana Patel
**PUBLISHING DIRECTOR** Megan Pearlman
**ASSOCIATE GENERAL COUNSEL** Helen Wan
**ASSISTANT DIRECTOR, SPECIAL SALES** Ilene Schreider
**SENIOR BRAND MANAGER** Nina Fleishman Reed
**ASSOCIATE PRODUCTION MANAGER** Kimberly Marshall
**ASSOCIATE PREPRESS MANAGER** Alex Voznesenskiy

**EDITORIAL DIRECTOR** Stephen Koepp
**SENIOR EDITOR** Roe D'Angelo
**GENERAL EDITOR** Christopher D. Hudson
**COPY CHIEF** Rina Bander
**DESIGN MANAGER** Anne-Michelle Gallero
**EDITORIAL OPERATIONS** Gina Scauzillo

**CONSULTING EDITORS**
Philip H. Towner, Ph.D.
Barbara Bernstengel, M.A.
Robert Hodgson, Ph.D.
Davina McDonald, M.A.
Thomas R. May, M.Div.

With special thanks to the American Bible Society's Committee
on Translation and Scholarship

**WRITERS**
Randy Southern
Selena Sarns
Christopher D. Hudson
Sammy Thale

**DESIGN AND PRODUCTION**
Mark Wainwright, Symbology Creative

**Special Thanks:** Katherine Barnet, Brad Beatson, Jeremy Biloon,
Dana Campolattaro, Susan Chodakiewicz, Rose Cirrincione, Natalie Ebel,
Assu Etsubneh, Christine Font, Susan Hettleman, Hillary Hirsch,
David Kahn, Amy Mangus, Nina Mistry, Dave Rozzelle, Ricardo Santiago,
Adriana Tierno

© 2014 Time Home Entertainment Inc.
Published by Time Home Entertainment Inc.
135 West 50th Street • New York, NY 10020

ISBN 10: 1-61893-367-1
ISBN 13: 978-1-61893-367-6

Unless otherwise noted, all Scripture quotations are
from the *Holy Bible, Contemporary English Version* (CEV).
Copyright 2006 by the American Bible Society. Used
by permission of the American Bible Society. All rights
reserved.

We welcome your comments and suggestions about
Time Home Entertainment Books. Please write to us at:
**Time Home Entertainment Books**
Attention: Book Editors
PO Box 11016
Des Moines, IA 50336-1016

If you would like to order any of our hardcover Collector's
Edition books, please call us at 1-800-327-6388,
Monday through Friday, 7 a.m. to 8 p.m., or Saturday,
7 a.m. to 6 p.m., Central Time.

**ART SOURCES**
Shutterstock
Thinkstock
iStock
Art Resource
Wikipedia

# Table of Contents

Ch 1.  Founding Mothers: Eight Women Who Shaped the Biblical Story ................................. 6
        Eve ................................................................................................................................. 8
        Job's Wife ..................................................................................................................... 11
        Sarah .............................................................................................................................. 13
        Hagar .............................................................................................................................. 16
        Keturah ........................................................................................................................... 19
        Rebekah .......................................................................................................................... 20
        Leah ................................................................................................................................. 22
        Rachel ............................................................................................................................. 26
Ch 2.  Women of Courage: Three Women Who Demonstrated Bravery in a Man's World ...... 28
        Jochebed ......................................................................................................................... 30
        Deborah .......................................................................................................................... 32
        Jael .................................................................................................................................. 34
Ch 3.  Walking Wounded: Four Women Who Endured Unimaginable Hardship ................... 38
        Dinah .............................................................................................................................. 40
        Jephthah's Daughter ....................................................................................................... 44
        Naomi .............................................................................................................................. 46
        Tamar .............................................................................................................................. 48
Ch 4.  The Chosen: Five Women Whose Names Appear in the Genealogy of Jesus ................. 50
        Tamar .............................................................................................................................. 53
        Rahab .............................................................................................................................. 54
        Ruth ................................................................................................................................. 58
        Bathsheba ....................................................................................................................... 60
        Mary ................................................................................................................................ 62
Ch 5.  The Prophets: Three Women Who Served as God's Messengers ................................... 64
        Miriam ............................................................................................................................. 67
        Huldah ............................................................................................................................. 68
        Anna ................................................................................................................................ 72
Ch 6.  Royalty: Seven Royal Women of the Old Testament ...................................................... 74
        Pharaoh's Daughter ........................................................................................................ 77
        Queen of Sheba ............................................................................................................... 78
        Vashti .............................................................................................................................. 82
        Esther .............................................................................................................................. 84
        Merab .............................................................................................................................. 86
        Michal .............................................................................................................................. 89
        Abigail ............................................................................................................................. 92

Ch 7.    Disappointed Dreamers: Three Women Who Discovered the Superiority
         of God's Plans................................................................................ 94

         Hannah................................................................................... 96
         Elizabeth................................................................................ 100
         Salome................................................................................... 102

Ch 8.    The Wicked: Four Women Who Embraced Evil ............................ 104

         The Medium of Endor................................................................ 106
         Jezebel................................................................................... 108
         Athaliah.................................................................................. 112
         Herodias................................................................................. 114

Ch 9.    Haunted Lives: Seven Women, the Choices They Made, and the Prices They Paid....... 116

         Lot's Wife............................................................................... 118
         Lot's Daughters ....................................................................... 122
         Delilah................................................................................... 124
         Maacah................................................................................... 126
         Gomer.................................................................................... 128
         Sapphira................................................................................. 130

Ch 10.   Fleeting Voices: Obscure Women of the Bible and Their Unlikely Impact.................... 132

         Zipporah ................................................................................ 134
         The Daughters of Zelophehad...................................................... 136
         Orpah.................................................................................... 140
         Abishag.................................................................................. 142
         Jehosheba............................................................................... 144

Ch 11.   Strange Encounters: Nine Women Who Met Jesus and Were Never the Same............. 146

         The Syrophoenician Woman........................................................ 148
         The Woman with an Illness ......................................................... 150
         Mary, Witness to the Crucifixion ................................................. 154
         Martha................................................................................... 157
         Mary of Bethany....................................................................... 158
         Joanna ................................................................................... 160
         The Samaritan Woman............................................................... 164
         The Woman Caught in Adultery.................................................... 166
         Mary Magdalene ...................................................................... 168

Ch 12.   The New Era Women: Eight Women Who Served the Early
         Church through Evangelism and Discipleship.................................. 170

         Dorcas.................................................................................... 172
         Mary, Mother of John Mark ........................................................ 175
         Lydia ..................................................................................... 178
         Bernice .................................................................................. 180
         Priscilla ................................................................................. 183
         Phoebe................................................................................... 184
         Eunice.................................................................................... 187
         Lois....................................................................................... 190

History and Mission of American Bible Society ........................................ 192

# INTRODUCTION

Their names are so revered in biblical history that they verge on legendary. They are women who were used by God to lay the groundwork for God's redemptive work in the world.

No one knows what Deborah was thinking when she led the Israelite forces into battle or why Rebekah chose to marry, sight unseen, a man whose father's servant decided she would be perfect for him. The most eminent theologian in the most ivy-covered seminary on the planet cannot say with absolute certainty how Zipporah felt about being married to Moses.

For better or worse, barring any stunning advances in time travel, guesswork will always play a role in the study of Bible characters. To examine the lives of people who lived in a time and culture radically different from our own is to walk a fine line. On the one hand, we must flesh out the characters in ways that are familiar and accessible to our modern sensibilities. On the other hand, we must be careful not to assign modern sensibilities to the characters themselves.

While the women of the Bible were restricted by their ancient culture in ways we can't fully comprehend, to pretend otherwise is to do a disservice to their stories—and to God's Word. The stories in this book show how many of them broke the mold and served God in unexpected ways. Yet every one of these women shared our human condition—and that grants us a kinship with them that connects us in a very real way. We can't know exactly what they thought and felt, but we can make informed guesses based on our own reactions and insights. More importantly, we can find very real inspiration and direction from their experiences.

Care must be taken, though, when approaching their stories from a literary perspective (as opposed to a theological or historical perspective). Toward that end, this book follows very specific guidelines in its fleshing-out process. First and foremost, the actual Bible narrative is treated as sacrosanct. The words of Scripture are presented exactly as they appear in the *Contemporary English Version*. No key details have been omitted for the sake of brevity or easier comprehension. Passages that seem to cast certain beloved "heroes of the faith"—and in some cases, even God himself—in a negative light have been left intact. It's better, after all, to wrestle with the thornier aspects of God's Word than to create an alternate version.

For the most part, speculation in this book is reserved for the women's motives, thoughts, and feelings regarding their experiences—emotions the Bible may or may not allude to. Some chapters will offer possible scenarios that may have preceded or followed the biblical narrative, but those scenarios are all very clearly marked as conjecture. That is to say, you'll have no trouble distinguishing which parts of the women's stories are divinely inspired.

The aim of this book is to present three-dimensional portraits of the women whose stories are told in Scripture—to connect, when possible, their experiences with ours and to discover the timeless and universal truths about God's interaction with his human creation.

# FOUNDING MOTHERS:
## Eight Women Who Shaped the Biblical Story

In a patriarchal world, women wielded enormous influence—first, in their roles as wives and mothers. They helped shape the men who shaped Israel.

Sarah advised Abraham and influenced Isaac. Rebekah advised Isaac and influenced Jacob. Rachel advised Jacob and influenced Joseph. The personalities, passions, and priorities of these history-shaping women were woven into the DNA of Israel.

Beyond their spousal and maternal roles, some of these women were active participants in God's covenant. They enjoyed personal relationships with God and played key roles in his plan. They were witnesses to his miraculous work.

Their fingerprints are all over the early biblical story.

Their near-mythical status is ironic when you consider that their portrayals in Scripture are robustly human. These were ordinary women placed in extraordinary circumstances. Their reactions to these circumstances—doubt, fear, laughter, hope, despair—are achingly familiar.

Yet God worked through each of them to achieve something remarkable and unprecedented. That should give hope to all who read their stories today.

chapter 1

In this chapter, we'll look at eight women whose lives still have the power to inspire and instruct:

- Eve, who understood perhaps better than anyone that unwise decisions can have unimaginable consequences
- Job's wife, whose agony clouded her perspective of God's nature
- Sarah, who worked through her doubt and experienced the wonders God can do
- Hagar, who found God's grace and protection under extreme conditions
- Keturah, who had the unenviable task of following Sarah as Abraham's wife yet still managed to carve her own niche in his life
- Rebekah, whose sense of adventure led her not only to the love of her life but also to playing a key part in God's plan
- Leah, who overcame her husband's rejection to play a central role in his family—and in the formation of Israel
- Rachel, the beloved wife of Jacob, whose competitive nature impacted her entire family

# Eve

## Did Eve ever recover from Eden?

O r did her sojourn there stay fresh in her mind until the day she died? Did the sights, sounds, and smells of paradise tantalize her memory decades after she experienced them? Or did it all fade like a half-remembered dream?

Did she talk with Adam about their garden days? Did they reminisce about the newness of creation? Did they laugh, remembering the joy and innocence of their nakedness? Did they share nostalgia for their favorite places in Eden, their favorite animals, their favorite fruits?

Or did Eve get quiet when the subject of fruit came up?

Did her heart ache when she remembered what it was like to stroll through the garden with God in the cool of the evening? Did her distance from him afterward leave her feeling lost and alone—even though she was with Adam?

Did she struggle with the consequences of her decision every day of her life? Did she ever get used to the difficult, unfulfilling work that consumed her waking hours? Did the pains of childbirth frighten her and break her heart in equal measure? Did she torture herself with constant thoughts of "If only . . ." and "How could I have . . . ?"

Did she tell her sons about what she had done? Did she accept responsibility for her actions?

Did she recognize that the path that led her away from God could also be taken back to him?

Did she test the waters of reconciliation with a few tentative prayers? Did her heart leap when she realized that forgiveness was possible? Did her soul feel lighter after she confessed what she'd done?

Did she continue to wrestle with feelings of shame and unworthiness in God's presence? Did her renewed relationship with him feel at all like her old one?

Did she turn to him for comfort and strength when tragedy struck? Did she pour out her grief to him when her son Abel was murdered? Did she ask God to help her make sense of her feelings toward her murderous son, Cain? Did she ask for protection for her wayward son?

Did Eve die with regrets? Or did she realize that God's love and forgiveness can overcome anything?

*Life Lesson:* **God can restore and renew all things.**

### One of a Kind

According to Genesis 2:21–22, Eve is unique among Bible characters. Besides Adam, who was created by God, every person born after Eve was born of a woman. Only Eve was born, so to speak, of a man.

The snake was sneakier than any of the other wild animals that the LORD God had made. One day it came to the woman and asked, "Did God tell you not to eat fruit from any tree in the garden?" The woman answered, "God said we could eat fruit from any tree in the garden, except the one in the middle. He told us not to eat fruit from that tree or even to touch it. If we do, we will die." "No, you won't!" the snake replied. "God understands what will happen on the day you eat fruit from that tree. You will see what you have done, and you will know the difference between right and wrong, just as God does." The woman stared at the fruit. It looked beautiful and tasty. She wanted the wisdom that it would give her, and she ate some of the fruit. Her husband was there with her, so she gave some to him, and he ate it too. At once they saw what they had done, and they realized they were naked. Then they sewed fig leaves together to cover themselves.

Genesis 3:1–7

Then Job sat on the ash-heap to show his sorrow. And while he was scraping his sores with a broken piece of pottery, his wife asked, "Why do you still trust God? Why don't you curse him and die?"

Job replied, "Don't talk like a fool! If we accept blessings from God, we must accept trouble as well." In all that happened, Job never once said anything against God.

# Job's Wife

## She mistook an intermission for an ending.

Fred Astaire is an icon of movie musicals—a dancer who epitomized grace and class. Partnered with Ginger Rogers, he could make even the most difficult routines look effortless.

Yet a comic-strip writer once pointed out that Ginger Rogers "did everything [Fred Astaire] did . . . backwards and in high heels" (*Frank and Ernest* comic strip, 1932).

A similar thing can be said of Job's wife. Job, after all, is well known as the unofficial patron saint of misery. Books have been written about the patience of Job, the trials of Job, the suffering of Job.

Yet Job's wife experienced the same devastation as her husband. She too lost all ten of her children. She too lost every bit of financial security. And when painful boils broke out all over her husband's body, whose job was it to comfort and care for him?

No friends came to comfort Job's wife in her misery. Nowhere in the book of Job do we find anyone trying to help her understand why a loving God would allow good people to suffer. While Job and his companions discussed and debated *ad nauseam*, Job's wife was left to wrestle with her own conclusions.

Job's wife came to believe that her husband had done something to displease God— something he may not even have been aware of—and that he was being punished for it. In her own memorably blunt way, she urged her husband to put an end to his suffering: "Why do you still trust God? Why don't you curse him and die?" (Job 2:9).

Those harsh words, spoken in desperation, likely haunted her for the rest of her life. Bible historians through the ages have used them to paint her as a pitiless shrew instead of as a hurting woman whose life had been turned upside down every bit as much as her husband's.

Perhaps it could be said that Job's wife made a miscalculation—the same mistake many of us make when we face devastation, loss, or some other crisis.

Job's wife mistook an intermission for an ending.

She concluded that her family's circumstances could not be changed—that what was true for her and her husband during one particular season would be true for the rest of their lives. She underestimated God's creative love for his people—his ability to bring something very, very good from something very, very bad.

Years later, Job's wife would have the opportunity to reflect on her experience in the comfort of her home—her financial security restored—surrounded by her husband and the ten children God blessed them with after their season of suffering had passed.

Where will you be and what will you have to celebrate when your season of suffering passes?

*Life Lesson:* **God is working out something beautiful in the midst of your suffering.**

11

## Dangerously Beautiful

Sarah was renowned for her extraordinary beauty. She was so beautiful, in fact, that it made her husband uneasy. When they traveled through foreign lands, Abraham was afraid the rulers of those lands would kill him and take Sarah for themselves. So he instructed her to tell people that she was his sister. Technically, that wasn't a lie. Sarah was Abraham's half sister, the daughter of Abraham's father, Terah.

# Sarah

*Obvious* is a relative term, where God is concerned. Sarah, the beloved wife of Abraham, learned this lesson the hard way.

On the face of things, the facts were plain:

- God had promised to make a great nation of Abraham's descendants.
- Sarah had been unable to conceive a child in her young adulthood.
- At the age of seventy-five, she was much too old to become a mother herself.
- Sarah had a servant named Hagar who was of childbearing age.

As far as Sarah could see, the obvious solution (and not an uncommon one in that day) was to have Abraham sleep with Hagar and get her pregnant. How else could God's promise be fulfilled?

It was so obvious.

Thus Sarah set her plan in motion, and Hagar became pregnant. Then something unexpected happened, something unplanned. Hagar, realizing she was giving Abraham the child Sarah couldn't provide, began to treat her mistress with contempt. Sarah responded in kind and became abusive toward her servant. The dysfunction continued long after Hagar gave birth—for fourteen more years, in fact.

Then God set his plan into motion. As it turns out, there was nothing obvious about it at all.

A trio of visitors arrived at Abraham's tent flap one day with a message: Sarah was going to give birth to a son—at the age of ninety. A son would be fathered by Abraham—at the age of one hundred.

This had been God's intention all along—to do something amazing, something that would set Abraham, Sarah, and their descendants apart from everyone else.

Sarah couldn't see this because she wasn't looking for it. She chose instead to take matters into her own hands and tried to force the Lord's hand by doing what seemed best to her.

The problem was that her limited imagination and perspective confined her to the realm of the obvious. She assumed the laws of the natural world governed God and his work.

How often do we make similar mistakes? How often do we find ourselves in a tight predicament and assume there's only one way out? How often do we try to force the Lord's hand with an obvious solution when he's capable of so much more? How often do we create unnecessary problems and complications for ourselves by believing we have God's will figured out?

*Life Lesson:* **God's view is better than ours. He will answer prayers in the best way and in the best time.**

For more on Sarah, read
Genesis 16, 18, 21.

THE LORD SAYS:

"MY THOUGHTS AND MY WAYS

ARE NOT LIKE YOURS.

JUST AS THE HEAVENS

ARE HIGHER THAN THE EARTH,

MY THOUGHTS AND MY WAYS

ARE HIGHER THAN YOURS."

ISAIAH 55:8–9

# Hagar

## The arrangement was destined to implode from the start.

Two women raising children fathered by the same man. In the same household.

When the inevitable tensions flared, Hagar, the servant, found herself with few options. She had no standing in the household, no leverage to use. Once upon a time, she'd been the mother of Abraham's only heir: her son Ishmael.

That changed the day Abraham's ninety-year-old wife, Sarah, gave birth to Isaac. In no time, Hagar and Ishmael's stock fell.

As the children grew older, it became apparent that the blended family was anything but. When Sarah caught Ishmael playing with Isaac, she reached her breaking point. She pleaded with Abraham to send Hagar and her son away—into the unforgiving desert.

Sarah's solution must have seemed especially cruel in light of the circumstances. The situation with Hagar and Ishmael was, after all, one of Sarah's own making. (It hadn't been Hagar's idea to sleep with Sarah's eighty-five-year-old husband.) Yet what could Hagar do?

Abraham prayed about the matter—and then agreed to his wife's plan. He gave Hagar and Ishmael a supply of bread and water and sent them to an uncertain fate.

Before long, the water ran out. With no hope left either, Hagar made Ishmael as comfortable as she could in the shade of a bush and then found a place for herself about a hundred yards away. She couldn't bear to watch her son die.

Hagar cried. Ishmael cried. Then an angel of God spoke from heaven.

> *Hagar, why are you worried? Don't be afraid. I have heard your son crying. Help him up and hold his hand, because I will make him the father of a great nation.* (Genesis 21:17–18)

Hagar noticed a nearby well that she hadn't seen before. She filled her container with water and gave Ishmael a drink. God's remarkable provision continued for two people who had been abandoned by society.

The narrative postscript mentions that Hagar found an Egyptian woman for Ishmael to marry and that they all settled in the Paran Desert. But that doesn't tell the whole story, nor does it fully convey the hope that Hagar's experience offers anyone who's been hurt, rejected, or abandoned.

The fact that God didn't rescue Hagar from her first predicament didn't mean he wasn't caring for her (see Genesis 16:1–16). Quite the opposite. He provided for Hagar in her desert experience (see Genesis 21:9–21). He gave her the strength to blossom in an inhospitable climate. He helped her to thrive where others might have wilted.

*Life Lesson:* **God hears our cries. Look for evidence of his provision in your life.**

**Genesis 16:1–6** *Abram's wife Sarai had not been able to have any children. But she owned a young Egyptian slave woman named Hagar, and Sarai said to Abram, "The LORD has not given me any children. Sleep with my slave, and if she has a child, it will be mine." Abram agreed, and Sarai gave him Hagar to be his wife. This happened after Abram had lived in the land of Canaan for ten years. Later, when Hagar knew she was going to have a baby, she became proud and treated Sarai hatefully.*

*Then Sarai said to Abram, "It's all your fault! I gave you my slave woman, but she has been hateful to me ever since she found out she was pregnant. You have done me wrong, and you will have to answer to the LORD for this."*

*Abram said, "All right! She's your slave—do whatever you want with her." Then Sarai began treating Hagar so harshly that she finally ran away.*

For more on Hagar, read Genesis 16, 21.

Genesis 25:1–6

## What's in a Title?

In some Bible translations, 1 Chronicles 1:32 refers to Keturah as a concubine—that is, a woman who fulfilled wifelike duties but did not enjoy all the privileges of marriage granted under the law.

*Abraham married Keturah, and they had six sons: Zimran, Jokshan, Medan, Midian, Ishbak, and Shuah. Later, Jokshan became the father of Sheba and Dedan, and when Dedan grew up, he had three sons: Asshurim, Letushim, and Leummim. Midian also had five sons: Ephah, Epher, Hanoch, Abida, and Eldaah.*

*While Abraham was still alive, he gave gifts to the sons of Hagar and Keturah. He also sent their sons to live in the east far from his son Isaac, and when Abraham died, he left everything to Isaac.*

# Keturah

## How could any other woman hope to measure up?

To become a second wife—to replace someone's spouse of many years—is difficult under the best of circumstances. The more fondly remembered (and dearly missed) the first wife is, the bigger the challenge the replacement wife faces.

A bit of respect is due for Keturah, the second wife of Abraham.

Her predecessor was Sarah. The Sarah of Genesis fame—the first woman mentioned in the "faith hall of fame" (see Hebrews 11:11). Sarah, the great love of Abraham's life. Sarah, the mother of his beloved son Isaac. Sarah, whose physical beauty drew the attention of kings.

How could any other woman hope to measure up?

Though the Bible is short on details, evidence suggests that Keturah managed quite well. Genesis 25:2 reveals that Keturah bore Abraham six sons. In a culture where children were practically currency, Keturah's fertility increased Abraham's stature dramatically.

God had promised Abraham descendants. Keturah, like Hagar and Sarah before her, played an active role in God's covenant. And she made a very real difference in her husband's life.

In her story, we find hope for second spouses everywhere. And though the Bible does not tell us how Keturah managed to find her own identity—how she escaped Sarah's shadow—there are a few principles worth remembering.

**1. The grieving process must be given its due.**
Whether a relationship ends in death, divorce, or permanent separation, it must be grieved. The process will vary from person to person, but it can't be rushed or skipped over. The more understanding and encouragement a second spouse can show for the grieving process, the better chance they have of beginning a relationship with an emotionally healthy partner.

**2. Avoid direct comparison.**
Competing with the memory of someone's first spouse is a fool's game. Even if the second partner compares favorably in certain areas, will it make up for the areas in which he or she falls short? No one in this situation should be lured into the trap of trying to be "better" than the first spouse.

**3. Maintain a strong sense of self.**
The second spouse must never lose sight of their God-given talents, strengths, and abilities. They must recognize that if anything were to happen to them (or their relationship), spouse number three would have enormous shoes to fill.

*Life Lesson: **Though you may feel like you never quite measure up, remember this: in God's eyes, you are his child.***

# Rebekah

## God rewarded her risks and sacrifices.

### Three Generations of Infertility: A Biblical Oxymoron

Like her mother-in-law, Sarah, before her and her daughter-in-law Rachel after her, Rebekah was unable to bear children for some time. When she finally became pregnant and gave birth to her twin sons, Esau and Jacob, it was recognized as God's miraculous answer to prayer.

The pitch was audacious, to say the least.

*I am Abraham's servant. . . . I solemnly promised my master that I would do what he said. And he told me, . . . go back to the land where I was born and find a wife for my son from among my relatives." . . .*

*When I came to the well today, I silently prayed, "You, LORD, are the God my master Abraham worships, so please lead me to a wife for his son while I am here at the well. When a young woman comes out to get water, I'll ask her to give me a drink. If she gives me a drink and offers to get some water for my camels, I'll know she is the one you have chosen." . . .*

*Now please tell me if you are willing to do the right thing for my master. Will you treat him fairly, or do I have to look for another young woman?* (Genesis 24:34–49)

What woman in her right mind would say yes?

A woman who understood the downside of staying in one's comfort zone, that's who.

Rebekah could have played it safe. No one would have blamed her for sticking with the life she knew best, the place she knew best, and the people she knew best. But playing it safe doesn't seem to have been Rebekah's style. Perhaps the thought of being stuck in one place—never knowing what she might have done or how far she might have gone—frightened her more than the unknown that comes with saying yes when opportunity knocks. Perhaps she sensed that true fulfillment lay far beyond her comfort zone.

Rebekah was a woman whose spirit of adventure could not be dulled by "what ifs."

What if her future husband turned out to be troll-like in appearance? What if he didn't find her attractive? What if she had trouble getting along with his family or fitting in with his people? Given time and a second-guessing nature, Rebekah might have talked herself out of her decision. Instead, she chose to trust her instincts and take a giant leap of faith.

Finally, Rebekah was a woman who understood that God delights in—and rewards—our risks and sacrifices.

Where God's plan is concerned, God's Spirit is at work. It's no stretch to believe that Rebekah heard God's voice—or at least felt a sense of peace from him about her decision. The question was, would she listen to God's prompting or allow practicality and cautiousness to guide her?

Every day with the Lord is an adventure. Those who enjoy it to the fullest are

- always up for a challenge;
- unafraid of a little risk;
- unattached to their comfort zones.

Rebekah was rewarded with a loving family, a life of adventure, a role in God's covenant, and a revered place in Jewish history.

What does God have in store for you?

*Life Lesson:* **Step out of your comfort zone and take a few risks with God. His ways are not our ways, but they are always good.**

For more on Rebekah, read Genesis 24.

# Leah

## The look of disappointment on Jacob's face must have stayed with Leah for the rest of her life.

He had expected to find Rachel in his wedding bed, not her older sister. Jacob had agreed to work for seven years for Laban in return for the honor of marrying his daughter Rachel.

Laban's decision to switch daughters at the last minute falls somewhere between a practical joke and outright fraud. Caught in the middle of Laban's deception was Leah.

Jacob's passion for Rachel was so great that he agreed to work another seven years for Laban in order to marry her. According to Genesis 29:31, "Jacob loved Rachel more than he did Leah." Are there more brutal words in all Scripture?

Yet Leah the Unloved persevered. She refused to accept her also-ran status. She asserted her rights and privileges as a wife. She couldn't make Jacob love her, but she could—and did—make herself an integral part of his life.

She bolstered her position as Jacob's wife by bearing and raising children. Producing heirs was vital to a man's standing in the ancient world. Unfortunately, Leah's sister Rachel was barren (or so it seemed).

Leah, the proverbial third wheel, suddenly had traction. In fact, she became very important to Jacob. She gave birth to six sons—representing half the twelve tribes of Israel—and one daughter. From Leah's third son, Levi, came

Israel's line of priests. From her fourth son, Judah, came Jesus, the Messiah. Clearly, Leah was no also-ran in God's eyes.

Have you ever been chosen last for a team, passed over for a promotion, overshadowed by a rival, made to feel like a second choice, or plagued by poor self-esteem? Anyone can take encouragement from Leah's story.

By reading between the lines in Genesis, we might even gather that Leah refused to be beaten down by the shortsightedness and indifference of others. She recognized her value in God's eyes and used that as the foundation for her self-image.

*Life Lesson:* **Your status is not what defines you. As God's child you are of great worth.**

**Genesis 29:21–25** *Jacob said to Laban, "The time is up, and I want to marry Rachel now!" So Laban gave a big feast and invited all their neighbors. But that evening he brought Leah to Jacob, who married her and spent the night with her. Laban also gave Zilpah to Leah as her servant woman.*

*The next morning Jacob found out that he had married Leah, and he asked Laban, "Why did you do this to me? Didn't I work to get Rachel? Why did you trick me?"*

For more on Leah, read Genesis 29.

## Honored in Death

Before his death, Jacob instructed his sons to bury his body in Machpelah Cave. This is where Abraham, Sarah, Isaac, and Rebekah had been buried (Genesis 49:29–31). This was also where Jacob chose to bury Leah. Rachel, however, had died in childbirth in Canaan and had to be buried during the course of the journey (35:19; 48:7).

*A truly good wife is the most precious treasure a man can find!*

*Proverbs 31:10*

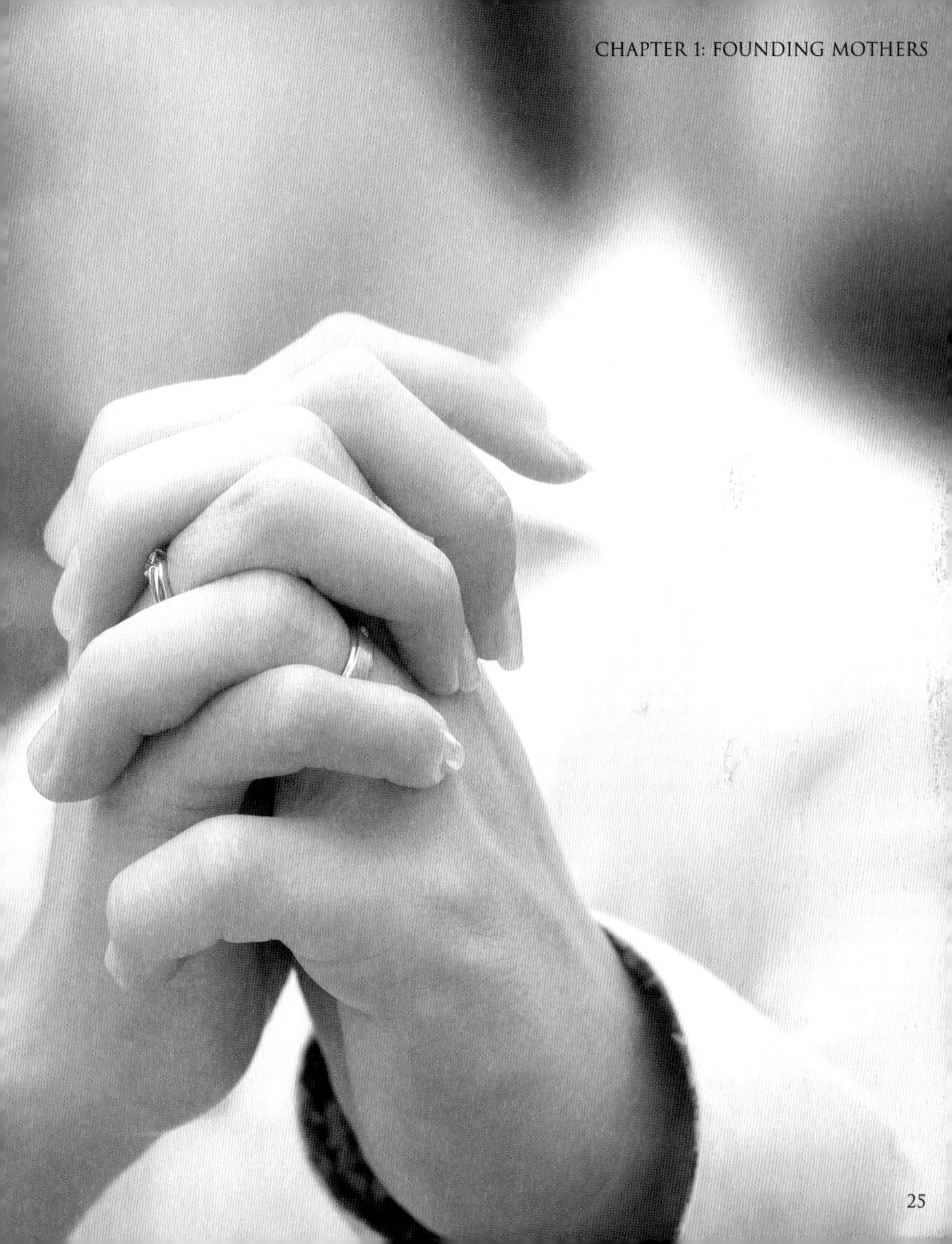

# Rachel

## The choices she made changed history.

Rachel had plenty of reasons to feel good about herself. She was quick-witted (see the "Like Father, Like Daughter" sidebar). She was attractive. (Her looks certainly turned Jacob's head.) She was loved. (Jacob worked seven years for her father just for the privilege of marrying her. When Rachel's father, Laban, deceived Jacob at the last moment, Jacob had to work seven more years for Rachel's hand.)

Yet Rachel couldn't find contentment. Her competitive spirit wouldn't allow it. The problem was her sister Leah, otherwise known as the wrench in the works.

On the night Rachel was to marry Jacob, Laban substituted her older sister, Leah, instead. Jacob didn't realize he'd been tricked until after the wedding night.

So Leah married Rachel's true love before Rachel did. Advantage: Leah.

After Jacob married Rachel too, he made it clear that he loved her, not Leah. Advantage: Rachel.

Still, Jacob split his husbandly duties between his two wives. In the course of those duties, Rachel discovered that she was barren. Leah, on the other hand, discovered that she was quite fertile. She gave birth to Reuben, Jacob's firstborn son; and Simeon, his second son; and Levi, his third son; and Judah, his fourth son. Advantage: Leah.

Rachel's competitive drive kicked into overdrive. Intensely jealous of her sister, she demanded that her husband give her children. Jacob retorted that God was the One who was keeping her from having children.

So Rachel switched strategies. She instructed Jacob to sleep with her servant Bilhah. Bilhah got pregnant—twice—and Rachel claimed each child as a victory for herself. She named Bilhah's first son Dan and the second son Naphtali.

If you're seeking insight into the character and motivation of Rachel, look no further than the meaning of the name Naphtali—"my struggle." Rachel said to herself, "I've struggled hard with my sister, and I've won!" (Genesis 30:8).

The advantage didn't last long. Leah insisted that Jacob sleep with her servant Zilpah—a relationship that produced two more sons.

## Like Father, Like Daughter

Rachel seems to have inherited a larceny gene from her father. As Jacob and his family were moving out of Laban's household, Rachel stole some of her father's idols and hid them in her camel's seat cushion.

Laban chased down Jacob's caravan and searched everyone and everywhere for his idols. Jacob, unaware of what Rachel had done, called down a curse of death on anyone who had the idols. When the time came to search Rachel's camel, she refused to climb down. She claimed she was having her period (Genesis 31:33–35).

Leah herself gave Jacob three more children— two sons and a daughter, for a total of seven.

Rachel finally countered with two children of her own: Joseph and Benjamin. So much for her diagnosis of infertility.

That's where the competition ended. Rachel left behind a husband and two sons. Her tumultuous life and seemingly premature death may cause us to ask several unanswerable questions:

- How much happier would her life have been if she'd been able to reconcile her competitive instincts with her better nature?
- What if she'd treated her sister like a teammate instead of as an opponent?
- What if all thirteen births in Jacob's family had been cause for celebration and not envy?
- What if Rachel had understood that competition and rivalry should bring out the best—not the worst—in people?

*Life Lesson:* **God can use ordinary, flawed people to change the course of history.**

For more on Rachel, read Genesis 29.

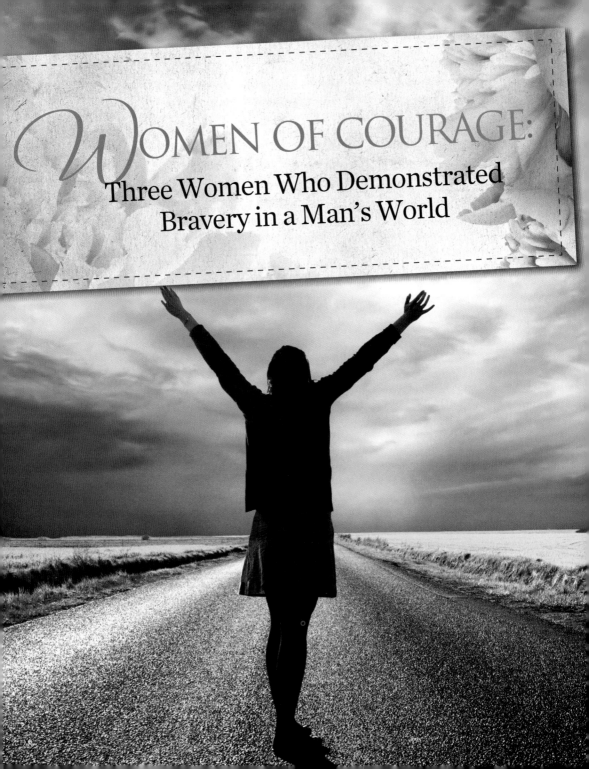

# WOMEN OF COURAGE:
## Three Women Who Demonstrated Bravery in a Man's World

The story of God's people is one of constant struggle.

Some of that struggle was by divine design—the conquest of Canaan, for example. The land had been promised to the descendants of Abraham, but it wasn't gift-wrapped and presented to them. The Israelites, a nomadic people not used to war, had to fight for their inheritance. Before they could claim the land as their own, they had to conquer and drive out the land's pagan occupants, people with better technologies, militaries, and economies.

Much of Israel's struggles, though, were needlessly self-inflicted. Chronic unfaithfulness was the main culprit. God's remedy was to allow the Israelites to suffer at the hands of their enemies until they cried out for help.

At critical points in Israel's history, then, God would raise a leader to seize the moment and turn the nation's focus back to him.

God's choices were eclectic to say the least. The people he called for leadership were a far cry from central casting. They were average, nondescript folks who—with divine prompting—looked deep within, found the courage and boldness that God had placed there, and acted decisively.

These unlikely heroes weren't born leaders; they were courageous leaders by circumstance. The one essential quality they all shared was a willingness to be used by God.

chapter 2

In this chapter, we'll look at three such women of courage:

- Jochebed, the mother of Moses, Aaron, and Miriam, whose bold example may have inspired her children to change the course of history
- Deborah, the prophet and judge who led Israel to a decisive victory against the Canaanites
- Jael, who outmaneuvered a Canaanite military commander in close quarters to put an end to twenty years of violent oppression

# Jochebed

## She boldly trusted God to work out the details in her life.

Nothing about Jochebed's humble origins hinted at the greatness that would come from her. She was born in captivity in Egypt. Her people were slave laborers. To keep the rapidly growing slave population under control, Pharaoh ordered that all Hebrew boys be put to death as soon as they were born.

Shortly thereafter, Jochebed gave birth to a baby boy.

Her older son, Aaron, had been born before Pharaoh's decree. Her daughter, Miriam, was unaffected, as the decree targeted boys. Jochebed's younger son, however, was caught in the crosshairs.

Desperate times call for desperate measures. So Jochebed crafted a waterproof basket for her newborn and placed him in the Nile River, near where Pharaoh's daughter regularly bathed. It was an audacious plan, but one that worked to perfection.

Pharaoh's daughter found the child and decided to keep him as her own. A strategically positioned Miriam offered to find a Hebrew woman to nurse and care for the baby, whom Pharaoh's daughter later named Moses.

Pharaoh's daughter, meet Jochebed.

Moses' quick-thinking mother was able to maintain a presence and influence in her son's life, even as he was raised by the Egyptian royal family. Eventually, that influence would rock Egypt to its core and help shift the balance of power in the ancient world.

Boldness and risk were hallmarks of Jochebed's life. Whether these characteristics were due to circumstances or personality is a matter of speculation. The Bible reveals little about Moses' mother.

What matters is that when her sons, Moses and Aaron, stood before Pharaoh to demand the release of the Hebrew people, they had Jochebed's example of boldness to draw on.

And when Moses and Aaron's sister, Miriam, joined her brothers in leading the entire Hebrew nation out of Egypt—away from Pharaoh's pursuing army, through a parted sea, across a vast wilderness, and toward an unknown destination in the face of constant opposition—she was already accustomed to risk, thanks to her mother.

Moses, Aaron, and Miriam were uniquely qualified to lead the Exodus from Egypt—in part, because they had a mother who was not content to play it safe.

*Life Lesson:* **We have no idea what God will do through our simple lives. Be willing to be bold and take risks, and trust God to work out the details.**

Exodus 2:1–10 *A man from the Levi tribe married a woman from the same tribe, and she later had a baby boy. He was a beautiful child, and she kept him inside for three months. But when she could no longer keep him hidden, she made a basket out of reeds and covered it with tar. She put him in the basket and placed it in the tall grass along the edge of the Nile River. The baby's older sister stood off at a distance to see what would happen to him.*

*About that time one of the king's daughters came down to take a bath in the river, while her servant women walked along the river bank. She saw the basket in the tall grass and sent one of them to pull it out of the water. When the king's daughter opened the basket, she saw the baby crying and felt sorry for him. She said, "This must be one of the Hebrew babies."*

*At once the baby's older sister came up and asked, "Do you want me to get a Hebrew woman to take care of the baby for you?"*

*"Yes," the king's daughter answered.*

*So the girl brought the baby's mother, and the king's daughter told her, "Take care of this child, and I will pay you."*

*The baby's mother carried him home and took care of him. And when he was old enough, she took him to the king's daughter, who adopted him. She named him Moses because she said, "I pulled him out of the water."*

Read Exodus 2

# Deborah

Her courage, decisiveness, and unwavering trust in God resulted in a military victory for her people.

The cycle was as predictable as the dry season in a desert. After a few years of obedience, the Israelites would forget God, ignore his laws, and dabble in idol worship. When their wickedness reached a critical point, God would send punishment—usually in the form of an enemy oppressor.

When the enemy's rule became unbearable, the Israelites would repent and ask God to send a deliverer to lead them against their enemy and out of oppression. Chastened and humbled, the Israelites would turn back to God—for a few years, anyway.

The pattern is repeated throughout the Old Testament. Only the players and the severity of the oppression change from one story to the next.

Around 1200 BC, the oppression grew nightmarish. The Israelites found themselves under the thumb of Jabin, the king of Canaan. Jabin's enforcer was a commander named Sisera, whose forces included 900 iron chariots. Sisera and his army wreaked havoc on the Israelites for two decades.

The Israelites needed a deliverer courageous enough to challenge Jabin and Sisera, and persuasive enough to rally the Israelite forces to battle.

Her name was Deborah.

Deborah was known as a prophet and a judge. People looked to her to settle their disputes. One day Deborah summoned a man named Barak and told him to assemble an army of ten thousand Israelites. The Lord, she said, was going to deliver the Canaanites into their hands.

The first words out of Barak's mouth reveal everything we need to know about Deborah: "I'm not going unless you go!"

Deborah's response is equally telling: "All right, I'll go!" she replied. "But I'm warning you that the LORD is going to let a woman defeat Sisera, and no one will honor you for winning the battle" (Judges 4:9).

On one level, it's a powerful subversion of the patriarchal culture of the day. On another level, it reveals the perspective that makes Deborah a role model to people everywhere. She was acutely aware of a "woman's place" in her society. But she was also acutely aware of her God-given gifts of leadership. She was not about to let the former interfere with the latter.

Under Deborah's leadership, Barak led the Israelites into battle against the Canaanites. When the fighting was done, not one soldier in Sisera's army was left alive.

Deborah did not let the shortsighted thinking of others keep her from trusting God or using her God-given gifts. As a result, she earned a revered place in Israel's history.

*Life Lesson: **Don't let others discourage you from using your God-given gifts. God can use those gifts to do something amazing through you.***

## Prophet, Judge, and Muse

Deborah is only one of three women in the Old Testament to have a poem ascribed to her (see Miriam's song in Exodus 15 and Hannah's prayer in 1 Samuel 2). Deborah's song in Judges 5 is considered one of the oldest texts in the Old Testament, possibly dating back to the twelfth century BC.

For more on Deborah, read Judges 4–5.

# Jael

## Of all the tents in all the plains in the entire ancient world, Sisera walked into hers.

Jael recognized him immediately. A ruthless Canaanite commander who had terrorized Israel for twenty years with an army of iron chariots is bound to make an impression. Gone, however, were his war machines and troops.

Sisera stood in Jael's tent, alone and vulnerable, yet still arrogant enough to demand her hospitality. Jael was only too eager to oblige. She ministered to the Canaanite's needs until he finally let down his guard. That's when she made her move. Using a hammer and a tent peg, Jael put Sisera out of Israel's misery.

Few will ever be called to do something as extreme as what Jael did. Yet anyone who aspires to be used by God can learn from her example.

**Jael recognized a heaven-sent opportunity when she saw it.**
God equips and prepares people to serve him. Jael may not have known exactly what he had in store for her, but she was ready when it came. Most people would have been startled or shaken by Sisera's intrusion. Jael seems to have recognized that God put her in the right place at the right time.

**Jael drew from a well of courage she may not have known she had.**
Sisera was a desperate, dangerous man. He was also a trained military commander. Killing people was part of his job description. Yet nowhere in the biblical narrative does it suggest that Jael was afraid of him. Such courage comes from God alone. Jael was smart enough to tap into it.

**Jael acted decisively.**
She didn't send for help. She didn't leave the job to someone more experienced or better suited for the role. She took action herself. As David—another unlikely warrior—would do years later, Jael grabbed the only weapons she could find and took down a monstrously intimidating foe.

Deborah, the Israelite prophet and judge who knew a thing or two about acting decisively when being used by God, celebrated Jael in song. In her words, we find the perfect epitaph for the woman who put an end to one of Israel's chief oppressors: "But honor Jael . . . give more honor to her than to any other woman" (Judges 5:24).

*Life Lesson:* **God has equipped and prepared you for a great purpose. Draw on his strength to accomplish the tasks he gives you, however extreme they might seem.**

## A Moral Dilemma

Jael's murderous action—though for a noble reason—violated ancient hospitality rules, especially given the peace treaty between her family and the Canaanites. This story is not just about being ready for an extreme task; it is far more seriously about great ethical and moral issues: justifiable homicide, oath and rule breaking, the principle of double effect (doing something inherently wrong for a larger good), and the role of individual conscience in moral judgment. In today's ethics, Sisera was an unarmed combatant, and Jael could have simply turned him in.

**Judges 4:16b–22** *Sisera's entire army was wiped out. Only Sisera escaped. He ran to Heber's camp, because Heber and his family had a peace treaty with the king of Hazor. Sisera went to the tent that belonged to Jael, Heber's wife. She came out to greet him and said, "Come in, sir! Please come on in. Don't be afraid."*

*After they had gone inside, Sisera lay down, and Jael covered him with a blanket. "Could I have a little water?" he asked. "I'm thirsty."*

*Jael opened a leather bottle and poured him some milk, then she covered him back up.*
*"Stand at the entrance to the tent," Sisera told her. "If someone comes by and asks if anyone is inside, tell them 'No.' "*

*Sisera was exhausted and soon fell fast asleep. Jael took a hammer and drove a tent-peg through his head into the ground, and he died.*

*Meanwhile, Barak had been following Sisera, and Jael went out to meet him. "The man you're looking for is inside," she said. "Come in and I'll show him to you."*

*They went inside, and there was Sisera—dead and stretched out with a tent-peg through his skull.*

*Jael Smote Sisera, and Slew Him,* James Jacques Joseph Tissot (1836–1902)

STRENGTH

FINALLY, LET THE MIGHTY STRENGTH OF THE LORD MAKE YOU STRONG. PUT ON ALL THE ARMOR THAT GOD GIVES, SO YOU CAN DEFEND YOURSELF AGAINST THE DEVIL'S TRICKS. WE ARE NOT FIGHTING AGAINST HUMANS. WE ARE FIGHTING AGAINST FORCES AND AUTHORITIES AND AGAINST RULERS OF DARKNESS AND POWERS IN THE SPIRITUAL WORLD. SO PUT ON ALL THE ARMOR THAT GOD GIVES. THEN WHEN THAT EVIL DAY COMES, YOU WILL BE ABLE TO DEFEND YOURSELF. AND WHEN THE BATTLE IS OVER, YOU WILL STILL BE STANDING FIRM.   EPHESIANS 6:10–13

# WALKING WOUNDED:

## Four Women Who Endured Unimaginable Hardship

Of the Bible's 1,189 chapters, only a handful are set before the fall. The rest detail God's interaction with a changed race of people. Sin's entrance into the world resulted in the inversion and perversion of everything God intended for us.

Once their fellowship with God was broken, wicked humans began to prey on one another. They inflicted intentional physical and emotional harm. They left broken, hurting people in their wake. The Bible is filled with their stories.

Of course, not all the victims in Scripture were treated wrongly by their fellow human beings. Some were wounded by the tragic loss of loved ones. Others suffered from serious illness or disability. Some were born into unfortunate or oppressive circumstances.

The wounded people in Scripture shared two things in common: the comfort they received from God's Spirit and the opportunities they had to witness his work firsthand.

To be clear, God does not cause people to inflict pain on one another in order to accomplish his work. He does, however, allow people to experience the consequences of living in a fallen world. And he works through and in the lives of hurting people to make himself known.

While it may seem that God does not always intervene to set things right, sometimes he works in the lives of wounded people to bring hope where none existed before. Sometimes he works in the wake of a cruel or vicious act to inspire righteous people to take action. Sometimes he uses an experience to emphasize the importance of remaining faithful to him.

# chapter 3

In this section, we'll look at four women whose lives were touched by tragedy or violence:

- Dinah, whose sexual assault triggered an extreme act of vengeance
- Jephthah's daughter, who paid the ultimate price for her father's rash words
- Naomi, who lost one family and gained another
- Tamar, King David's daughter, whose life was ruined by someone close to her

Their stories offer valuable clues as to how God might work in and through our lives when we are wounded.

# Dinah

"No good deed goes unpunished."

Based on a
True Story
The best-selling 1997 novel
*The Red Tent* by Anita
Diamant is a fictionalized
account of Dinah's story.

Surely this phrase (or its nearest Hebrew equivalent) occurred to Dinah in the aftermath of the attack. She had been visiting other young women near her campsite, building friendly relations with her family's neighbors in Canaan.

That's what she was doing when Shechem, the prince of the region, spotted her, seized her, and raped her.

After the assault, the royal sex offender tried to romance Dinah with tender words. He believed he could win her heart even after he'd forced himself on her. Shechem pleaded with his father, King Hamor, to arrange a marriage with Dinah.

Hamor pitched the idea to Dinah's father, Jacob, and her brothers. The brothers, who knew what Shechem had done to Dinah, agreed to the marriage under one condition: Shechem, along with every man in his family and every man in his hometown, had to be circumcised first.

Shechem and his compatriots jumped at the offer. They were eager to intermarry with Jacob's family and claim its wealth for their own. So every man in town went under the knife. Three days later, while they were still recovering from the procedure, two of Dinah's brothers, Simeon and Levi, showed up with swords in their hands and payback on their minds.

None of the townsmen were in any condition to put up a fight. Simeon and Levi slaughtered every last man. Dinah's other brothers joined in to plunder the town, taking the women and children as captives.

Dinah belonged to a culture in which revenge— "life for life, eye for eye, tooth for tooth" (Exodus 21:23–24)—ruled tribal relations. Avenging their family's honor was the driving force behind Dinah's brothers' rampage.

If Dinah received any comfort, it came from God's Spirit, not from her brothers' violent outrage. Passages such as Genesis 28:15 make clear that God is our ultimate source of comfort and protection.

In fact, Dinah's brothers' reprisal may have interfered with the healing process. Imagine the conflicting emotions Dinah may have felt: sadness over the misery inflicted on those who had nothing to do with her assault, unfounded guilt over her complicity in those deaths, anger at her brothers for making an already horrible situation even worse.

Vengeance is a weapon too dangerous for human understanding. Our idea of revenge cannot solve a problem; it can only escalate it.

*Life Lesson:* **God sees what we sometimes can't. He is loving and just. Leave vengeance to him.**

*Genesis 34:1–7 Dinah, the daughter of Jacob and Leah, went to visit some of the women who lived nearby. She was seen by Hamor's son Shechem, the leader of the Hivites, and he grabbed her and raped her. But Shechem was attracted to Dinah, so he told her how much he loved her. Shechem even asked his father to arrange for him to marry her.*

*Meanwhile, Jacob heard what had happened. But his sons were out in the fields with the cattle, so he did not do anything at the time. Hamor arrived at Jacob's home just as Jacob's sons were coming in from work. When they learned that their sister had been raped, they became furiously angry, because nothing is more disgraceful than rape, and it must not be tolerated.*

For more on Dinah, read Genesis 34.

ROMANS 12:18-19

*Do your best to live at peace with everyone. Dear friends, don't try to get even. Let God take revenge. In the Scriptures the Lord says, "I am the one to take revenge and pay them back."*

# Jephthah's Daughter

## "Sticks and stones may break my bones, but words will never hurt me."

The Old Testament book of Judges introduces a young woman who would have laughed bitterly at this taunt. Indeed, sticks and stones might have dealt her a much kinder fate, given the chance.

The woman's name is never given, but her father was Jephthah, a mighty warrior. The people of Gilead recruited Jephthah to help them fight against the Ammonites. In return, they promised to make him their ruler.

On the eve of battle, Jephthah made a vow to God. He didn't need to. The Lord was already on his side. Victory was guaranteed. What's more, the Lord took vows very seriously.

Still Jephthah wanted some extra insurance. So he vowed that if God would give him victory, he would sacrifice the first thing that ran out to greet him when he returned home.

The Bible doesn't say who or what he expected to greet him. (A sheep? A bird?) It turned out to be his daughter. His only child.

Jephthah was devastated. He had no choice but to follow through on his promise. A vow to God, even one foolishly made, was considered sacred.

Even Jephthah's daughter understood that. Human sacrifice was not unfamiliar to her. She submitted herself quietly to the ritual because it was part of the customs of her time (Leviticus 18:21). She asked only to be given two months to roam the hills with her friends and mourn the fact that she would never experience motherhood. When she returned, Jephthah sacrificed her to fulfill his vow.

Their story offers a stark reminder of how careless words can harm others. Granted, the fate of Jephthah's daughter was extreme. Yet the point remains: words have power to cut a wide swath of damage through people's lives.

*Life Lesson: Words are powerful and can build up or destroy. Choose your words carefully.*

For more on Jephthah's daughter, read Judges 11.

## A Fate Better Than Death

Some Bible scholars believe Jephthah's daughter may not have ended up as a human sacrifice, after all. They point to the references that emphasize her virginity to suggest that her "sacrifice" may have involved a lifetime of service at the tabernacle, which would have required her to remain celibate.

# Naomi

A widow's lot in the patriarchal world of Scripture was not pleasant.

For more on Naomi, read Ruth 1–4.

Naomi had good reason to worry when her husband Elimelech died.

When her sons Mahlon and Chilion followed their father to an early grave, Naomi had reason to suspect that God's hand was turned against her. A childless widow in the ancient world dwelled at the bottom fringes of society, trapped in poverty, despair, and neglect.

Naomi's grief was bitter indeed. As an Israelite, she was a stranger in a strange land. Before dying, Elimelech had moved the family to the neighboring country of Moab. Naomi was alone, save for her daughters-in-law—the Moabite wives her sons had taken before their deaths.

Naomi decided her only option was to return to her people in Judah. A sense of loyalty and duty compelled her daughters-in-law, Orpah and Ruth, to follow her. Naomi reminded them that her homeland held no promise for them. She released Orpah and Ruth from their obligations to her and urged them to return to their own land and their own people.

Orpah did so, but Ruth insisted on staying with Naomi. Once again Naomi urged Ruth to leave and return to her homeland, little realizing Ruth would become God's instrument of redemption and hope in her life.

Ruth wouldn't hear of it, so together the two women traveled to Judah. The homecoming brought Naomi no relief. Lest any of her old acquaintances mistake her for the happy person she'd been when she left, she insisted they call her Mara, which means "bitter."

Life in Judah was difficult until Naomi and Ruth met Boaz, a wealthy relative of Naomi's dead husband, Elimelech. To make a long story short, Boaz bought a parcel of land that belonged to Naomi (and her late husband). In that culture, the transaction required him to marry Ruth and sire a son who would carry on Naomi and Ruth's family name. So together they made a home.

There's a lesson in Naomi's story for anyone who's ever lost family members, whether through death or estrangement. When your biological relatives are gone, the people who remain by your side when you need them most—the ones who love and support you unconditionally and who want only the best for you—become your family.

Embrace them. Treasure them. Return their loyalty. Treat them like the heaven-sent gifts they are.

*Life Lesson:* **When it seems there is no solution to your problems, trust God to provide a clear answer.**

## A Child Is Born

Naomi quickly warmed to life as a grandmother—a role she once thought she'd never experience. Naomi helped care for Ruth and Boaz's son Obed. In fact, Naomi and Obed were so close that the women of Judah called Obed "Naomi's Boy" (Ruth 4:17).

*Naomi Entreating Ruth and Orpah to Return to the Land of Moab,* William Blake (1757–1827)   47

# Tamar

## She endured a life of loneliness after being objectified, victimized, and ostracized.

Dysfunction was rampant in King David's family. That's bound to be the case when your household is an unnatural blend of assorted wives and offspring. For one son, though, dysfunction morphed into obsession—and eventually into sexual violence.

Amnon was his name. He was the half brother of David's daughter Tamar. Amnon convinced himself that he was in love with his half sister. So intense were his feelings that he became physically ill with lust.

With the help of his despicable cousin, Amnon concocted a scheme to satisfy his obsession. He made a show of his illness. When his father came to check on him, Amnon asked the king to send Tamar to care for him.

Ever the dutiful daughter and concerned sister, Tamar hurried to Amnon's house to help. She prepared his favorite dish and brought it to him. She must have sensed something wasn't right when her half brother sent his servants away and asked her to feed him in his bedroom. Before she could object, "he grabbed her and said, 'Come to bed with me!'" (2 Samuel 13:11).

The quick-thinking Tamar appealed to Amnon's rational thinking. She warned him what would happen to his standing in the kingdom if he forced himself on her. By that time, though, Amnon was beyond the grip of rational thought. Having objectified Tamar for so long, he raped her in his bedroom.

After the assault, Amnon had a sudden change of heart. Likely projecting his own self-loathing on his victim, he immediately felt hatred toward Tamar and demanded that she leave.

Amnon's cruelty was a second violation of Tamar. No longer a virgin, her prospects for marriage were virtually nonexistent in the ancient world. As unthinkable as it seems today, her only hope for a "normal" life back then would have been to marry her rapist half brother. Yet Amnon denied her even that meager consolation.

"Tamar soon moved into Absalom's house, but she was always sad and lonely" (2 Samuel 13:20). The end.

What a heartbreaking epilogue to what had been such a promising life.

Tamar was let down by the very people who should have been looking out for her: her half brother, who ignored the destructive danger in his twisted desires; a cousin, who failed to warn Tamar about her half brother's obsession; her father, who unwittingly facilitated the attack.

Tamar's family failed her just as miserably after the rape. King David became angry when he heard about Amnon's heinous crime, but he did nothing. Tamar's brother Absalom took Tamar in, but he allowed his own anger to overshadow her pain. Two years later, Absalom killed Amnon.

Tamar's experience drives home the importance of not failing those in our lives who have been subjected to sexual assault—and of leaning on God to make us whole when the unthinkable happens.

*Life Lesson: God does not promise life will be easy, but he does promise he will be with us when difficult things happen.*

**2 Samuel 13:1–4** *David had a beautiful daughter named Tamar, who was the sister of Absalom. She was also the half sister of Amnon, who fell in love with her. But Tamar was a virgin, and Amnon could not think of a way to be alone with her. He was so upset about it that he made himself sick.*

*Amnon had a friend named Jonadab, who was the son of David's brother Shimeah. Jonadab always knew how to get what he wanted, and he said to Amnon, "What's the matter? You're the king's son! You shouldn't have to go around feeling sorry for yourself every morning."*

*Amnon said, "I'm in love with Tamar, my brother Absalom's sister."*

For more on Tamar, read 2 Samuel 13.

# THE CHOSEN:
## Five Women Whose Names Appear in the Genealogy of Jesus

In biblical times, a genealogy was central to a person's identity. Ancestry was so important in Jewish culture that those who could not prove their lineage were considered outsiders.

God's people took pride in being able to trace their family lines through the tribes of Israel, all the way back to Abraham himself. To be able to claim David or some other Hebrew notable as a direct ancestor was a matter of great honor.

Of course, where there are ancestors, there are descendants. And the people of Israel did everything in their power to make sure their descendants brought them as much honor as their ancestors.

Without question, the most prestigious descendant of all was the Messiah—the Savior, God's Chosen One. To be included in the messianic line was to be mentioned in the same breath as the Savior, to be connected to him as family.

What would a person have to do to be accorded such an honor? How impeccable would her credentials need to be? The answer may surprise you.

chapter 4

In this chapter, we'll look at five women who won the genealogical sweepstakes—five women who were chosen by God to be direct ancestors of his Son, five women whose names appear in the genealogy of Jesus:

- Tamar, Judah's daughter-in-law, whose controversial tactic for claiming her rights as a widow helped her to continue the lineage of Judah
- Rahab, the prostitute whose fearless actions on behalf of the Israelites garnered her a place not only in their history but in the ancestry of the Messiah
- Ruth, whose faithful sacrifice went unnoticed by almost everyone but God
- Bathsheba, who overcame scandal and tragedy to become the wife of one king and mother of another
- Mary—blessed among women, yet humble to the core—who gave birth to the Savior

**Genesis 38:6–11** *Later, Judah chose Tamar as a wife for Er, his oldest son. But Er was very evil, and the LORD took his life. So Judah told Onan, "It's your duty to marry Tamar and have a child for your brother." Onan knew the child would not be his, and . . . he made sure that she would not get pregnant. The LORD wasn't pleased with Onan and took his life too. Judah did not want the same thing to happen to his son Shelah, and he told Tamar, "Go home to your father and live there as a widow until my son Shelah is grown." So Tamar went to live with her father.*

For more on Tamar,
read Genesis 38.

# Tamar

## She refused to let go of what had been promised to her.

In a culture where she had no voice, in a system stacked entirely against her, Tamar managed to outwit one of the fathers of the twelve tribes of Israel. In the process, she secured a place in the lineage of the Messiah.

Tamar first met Judah when he chose her to marry his oldest son, Er. Er turned out to be a bad guy—so evil that God struck him dead before he could father a child with Tamar.

According to the Levirate tradition of the day (Deuteronomy 25:5–6), the task of producing an heir was passed to Judah's middle son, Onan, who was no prize either. Since the first son born to Tamar would have been considered Er's, Onan felt he had nothing to gain from the coupling. So he shirked his procreative duties, for which God struck him down too.

That left Judah's youngest son, Shelah. By this time, though, Judah was convinced that Tamar was cursed. He told her Shelah was too young to marry. Judah sent Tamar back to her family with the promise that when Shelah was old enough, he would marry her.

Judah lied.

Tamar took matters into her own hands. One day, when she heard Judah was traveling to a place called Timnah, she disguised herself with a veil and sat beside the road. When Judah passed by, he assumed the veiled woman was a prostitute. So he propositioned her.

### From Shame to Honor

Judah and Tamar committed an act that was sinful in the eyes of God. Yet both their names appear in the genealogy of Christ (Matthew 1:3).

They negotiated a price of one goat. As a show of good faith, Judah gave Tamar his identification seal and cord and his walking stick. They consummated their arrangement, and Judah went on his way, unaware that he'd just had sex with his daughter-in-law.

Later, when Judah sent one of his friends to deliver the goat, the woman was gone—and no one seemed to know who she was.

Three months later, Judah received some disturbing news. His former daughter-in-law had behaved like a prostitute and gotten pregnant. Full of indignation (and empty of any sense of hypocrisy), Judah demanded that Tamar be burned to death.

That's when Tamar showed Judah the seal, the cord, and the walking stick. Caught in his own hypocrisy, Judah conceded, "She's a better person than I am" (Genesis 38:26).

Tamar gave birth to twins, one of whom became a direct ancestor of Jesus, the Messiah. God rewarded Tamar for refusing to let go of what had been promised her.

*Life Lesson: If you hold fast to God's promises, you will be blessed.*

# Rahab

## She risked her life to save her family.

The Israelites stood poised to attack the walled city of Jericho. Yet their leader Joshua was not quite ready to issue marching orders. Ever the careful strategist, he first sent two spies into the city to scope out its military capabilities.

The spies took shelter in the house of Rahab, a local prostitute. Enemy soldiers caught wind of the spies' presence and surrounded Rahab's house. They demanded that Rahab turn over the spies to them. (Ancient custom prohibited men from entering a woman's house without being invited, and Rahab wasn't sending out invitations.)

In an extraordinary move, Rahab told the soldiers that the spies had already escaped. (They were actually hidden under bundles of flax on her roof.) The soldiers believed her and left. The grateful spies instructed Rahab to hang a red rope out of her window on the day of the assault. When the Israelites laid waste to the city and its inhabitants, the rope would identify Rahab and her family as allies, and they would be spared.

Needless to say, if Rahab had been caught sheltering the spies, the consequences would have been severe. Why would Rahab risk everything for a cause she knew nothing about?

Based on the biblical narrative, there are at least two possible explanations. One, Rahab stood in awe of God's power—which is more than many of the Israelites could say. She had heard the stories of God parting the Red Sea (and other miracles) and realized that she needed to be on his side.

**Joshua 2:8–14a** *Rahab went back up to her roof. The spies were still awake, so she told them: "I know that the LORD has given Israel this land. Everyone shakes with fear because of you. We heard how the LORD dried up the Red Sea so you could leave Egypt. . . . We know that the LORD your God rules heaven and earth, and we've lost our courage and our will to fight. Please promise me in the LORD's name that you will be as kind to my family as I have been to you. Do something to show that you won't let your people kill my father and mother and my brothers and sisters and their families." "Rahab," the spies answered, "if you keep quiet about what we're doing, we promise to be kind to you when the LORD gives us this land."*

For more on Rahab, read Joshua 2.

Two, she was asked. The God of the Israelites chose Rahab, a prostitute, to play a key role in his plan. Imagine the enormous effect that must have had on a woman who'd likely been treated as an outcast for most of her life. Pushed to the margins of her own society, Rahab found worth in God's eyes.

Perhaps that's what gave her the courage to risk everything and betray her own people—a betrayal that brought victory to Israel and destruction to her city. Perhaps that explains why she escaped the destruction of Jericho. Perhaps that explains why Rahab became part of the messianic line.

*Life Lesson: **Any risk you take for God will pale in comparison to his reward.***

## Royal Blessing

According to Matthew 1:5–6, Rahab ended up marrying an Israelite. Their great-great-grandson was none other than King David.

The Lord is good.
He protects those who trust
him in times of trouble.

Nahum 1:7

## A True Friend

The Hebrew word for *Ruth* means "friendship" or "companion." Ruth's friendship and loyalty to her mother-in-law serve as themes throughout the entire book of Ruth.

# Ruth

## She chose self-sacrifice over self-preservation.

The situation was dire. Naomi had lost her husband and her only two sons. Her daughters-in-law, Orpah and Ruth, had lost their husbands. The three women were not only emotionally devastated but also physically vulnerable. Gone was any sense of security or well-being they may have had. In a patriarchal culture and with no husbands or sons to provide for them, they were at the mercy of others.

Naomi, an Israelite living in Moab, decided to return to her homeland to live out her final years. Orpah and Ruth, both Moabites, offered to accompany her; but Naomi knew she had no future to offer them, so she urged them to remain in Moab with their own people.

Orpah and Ruth weighed their options carefully. Their very futures were at stake. Orpah decided her best course of action was to stay in Moab. Perhaps she hoped to find a new husband there.

Ruth chose to accompany Naomi to Judah.

When self-preservation was the safe play, Ruth chose self-sacrifice instead. Her motivation was to do the right thing, whether it benefited her or not. Perhaps Ruth could sense that Naomi was teetering on the brink of severe depression. Perhaps Ruth was concerned that Naomi wouldn't be able to take care of herself. Whatever the reason, Ruth set aside her own preferences, her own comfort, and her own hopes for the future in order to make life more bearable for Naomi.

In Judah, the two women struggled to survive—that is, until they met Boaz, a wealthy relative of Naomi's late husband. In keeping with ancient tradition, Boaz agreed to buy land that belonged to Naomi. As part of the transaction, he also agreed to marry Ruth and continue Naomi's family line. Among the descendants of Ruth and Boaz was the Messiah.

Back in Moab, Ruth stood to gain nothing from her sacrificial decision. Ruth made sure that Naomi was taken care of, and in turn God made sure that Ruth was taken care of.

*Life Lesson: God takes care of those who take care of others.*

*Ruth 1:14–18 Orpah kissed her mother-in-law goodbye, but Ruth held on to her. Naomi then said to Ruth, "Look, your sister-in-law is going back to her people and to her gods! Why don't you go with her?"*

*Ruth answered,*

*"Please don't tell me*
*to leave you*
  *and return home!*
*I will go where you go,*
  *I will live where you live;*
*your people will be my people,*
  *your God will be my God.*
*I will die where you die*
  *and be buried beside you.*
*May the LORD punish me*
*if we are ever separated,*
  *even by death!"*

For more on Ruth, read Ruth 1-4.

*When Naomi saw that Ruth had made up her mind to go with her, she stopped urging her to go back.*

# Bathsheba

## Her resilience and faith grew in the midst of suffering and scandal.

The message from King David wasn't an invitation; it was a summons. Bathsheba had no choice but to comply. With her husband, Uriah, away on a military campaign, there was no one else to speak up for her, no one else to put a stop to what the king had in mind.

It likely wasn't the first time Bathsheba's beauty had attracted unwanted attention. Perhaps she clung to hope that King David—God's chosen leader of Israel—wasn't that type of man, that he hadn't really been spying on her while she bathed, that he had too much integrity to take advantage of the wife of one of his most loyal soldiers.

How her heart must have sunk when her worst fears were confirmed.

How terrified she must have been a few weeks later when she had to tell the king that she was pregnant with his child.

If God works through bad situations to bring about good things, he had plenty of raw material to work with in Bathsheba's life. Perhaps it was this hope—the conviction that God would ultimately make things better—that motivated Bathsheba to carry on.

Throughout Bathsheba's relationship with King David, she endured

- being violated;
- carrying the child of the man who violated her;
- losing her husband who died in battle;
- losing her newborn son.

If Bathsheba's faith in God was so strong that she believed something good would come from these circumstances, then she was right.

Soon after David married Bathsheba, God allowed their newborn son, who was conceived in their adulterous affair, to become sick and die. Bathsheba eventually gave birth to three other sons. In so doing, she became part of the messianic line. Her name appears in the genealogy of Jesus as the mother of Solomon.

When David was very old, Bathsheba worked with the prophet Nathan to ensure that God's chosen successor to the throne—her son Solomon—inherited the crown. She outmaneuvered various factions built around David's other sons to secure Solomon's historic reign and usher in Israel's golden age.

From helpless victim to political power player, Bathsheba is a testament to the power of endurance and faith.

*Life Lesson:*
*If you stay close to God, you can endure any tragedy or setback—and emerge stronger from its wake.*

I will never give up hope
or stop praising you.
All day long I will tell
the wonderful things you do
to save your people.
But you have done much more
than I could possibly know.
I will praise you, Lord God,
for your mighty deeds
and your power to save.

PSALM 71:14–16

# Abigail

Her boldness, wisdom, and quick thinking prevented disaster.

The Bible doesn't say how Nabal and Abigail became a couple, but blackmail is a pretty good guess. Or kidnapping. Or perhaps an extremely large sum of money paid to Abigail's family. No other explanation makes sense.

Abigail was something special. The author of 1 Samuel purposefully described her as "sensible and beautiful." The Talmud refers to her as "one of four women of surpassing beauty in the world." What's more, a quick read of 1 Samuel 25 suggests that Abigail's physical attributes may have paled in comparison to her intelligence, diplomacy, and crisis-management skills.

Nabal, on the other hand, was a virtual Neanderthal. The author of 1 Samuel intentionally described him as "rough and mean." In Hebrew, *Nabal* actually means "fool" (1 Samuel 25:25).

To get a glimpse of Nabal's foolish character, you need look no further than 1 Samuel 25. David and his band of 600 warriors were on the run from Saul near the town of Carmel, where Abigail and Nabal lived. While staying there, David's men kept an eye on a large flock of sheep owned by Nabal. David and his warriors protected Nabal's shepherds and his sheep from harm.

One day David sent messengers to Nabal, asking if he could spare some provisions. Not only did Nabal refuse David's request but he went out of his way to taunt, embarrass, and humiliate the future king.

One of Nabal's servants, who overheard the exchange, knew exactly what to do: run to Abigail and tell her everything. Abigail sprang into action immediately. She gathered two hundred loaves of bread, two large jars full of wine, five slaughtered sheep, a large sack of roasted grain, one hundred handfuls of raisins, and two hundred handfuls of dried figs, and she rode out to deliver them to David.

She arrived just as David and his men were preparing to attack Nabal and all the male members of his household. Abigail bowed to David and apologized for her husband's abhorrent behavior. She appealed to David's conscience. She also predicted a lasting dynasty for David, one that would rule Israel for generations.

Abigail knew exactly how to appease David's anger. Her genuine concern, not only for her own household but also for David's legacy, moved the future king to call off his attack.

Abigail returned home to find Nabal hosting a drunken party. Typical. She waited until the next morning, after he'd sobered up, to tell him what she'd done. Nabal had a heart attack on the spot. Ten days later, he died.

When David received word of Nabal's death, he immediately asked Abigail to marry him. Abigail accepted his proposal and became the wife of the king of Israel.

*Life Lesson: **Embrace every opportunity to use your God-given gifts and abilities to boldly promote behavior that is pleasing to God.***

## It Takes a Strong Woman

Abigail endured more than just marriage to a foolish first husband. Life with David was dangerous—when the Amalekites burned David's city of Ziklag, they kidnapped Abigail, along with all the children and women (1 Samuel 30:1–20). Life with David was complicated—Abigail shared her husband with many other wives. Life with David brought conflict—many wives led to many sons (2 Samuel 3:2–5), and many sons fought to claim their father's throne.

For more on Abigail, read 1 Samuel 25.

# DISAPPOINTED DREAMERS:

## Three Women Who Discovered the Superiority of God's Plans

Misguided expectations are the leading cause of disappointment—in Scripture, as well as in everyday life. When our expectations aren't grounded in reality, or in an actual understanding of God and his will, disappointment is inevitable. How we deal with that disappointment sets the tone for our relationship with God.

The expectations that lead to disappointment can be divided into two categories. First, there are the self-generated expectations. We look around at God's blessings in the lives of other people, conclude that what's true for them must be true for us too, and adjust our outlook accordingly.

Sometimes those expectations are driven by a naive view of God and his work: *He wants me to be happy, but I'll only be happy if this happens. Therefore, God will make this happen.* Sometimes they're driven by greed, narcissism, or a sense of entitlement. Either way, the result is the same. (Although, in Scripture, greedy, entitled narcissists tend to get a heaping helping of comeuppance in addition to their disappointment.)

In the second category are expectations perpetuated by society. Such cultural expectations were especially insidious for women in ancient times who were unable to bear children. Sarah and Rachel (whose stories are told in the first chapter of this book) felt the sting of cultural expectations regarding motherhood. They're in good company.

chapter 7

In this chapter, we'll look at three women whose lives were significantly influenced by misguided expectations:

- Hannah, the mother of Samuel, who weathered disappointment and humiliation for years until God answered her prayers for a son
- Elizabeth, the mother of John the Baptist, who spent her child-bearing years barren, only to get pregnant in her old age
- Salome, the wife of Zebedee and the mother of James and John, whose wildly ambitious plans for her sons were dashed by Jesus himself

These disappointed dreamers discovered that God will not be manipulated by human expectations. In fact, more often than not, God prefers to defy those expectations in order to demonstrate the superiority of the divine plan and will.

# Hannah

She refused to let go of her dream.

Hannah must have cut a pitiful figure. Barren in a culture that prized fertility, she was essentially a "marked" woman—an object of shame, scorn, and speculation.

"The LORD had kept her from having children of her own" (1 Samuel 1:5). That was the prevailing diagnosis. Physiology? Forget about it. As far as the people around her were concerned, the issue was spiritual, not physical. God had refused to allow Hannah to bear children. Let the tongues wag.

As if that weren't bad enough, Hannah shared her home—and her husband, Elkanah—with a second wife. The difference between the two women is indelicately summarized in 1 Samuel 1:2: "Although Peninnah had children, Hannah did not have any."

Every day Hannah was reminded of her childless condition. Peninnah made sure of that. She preyed on Hannah's vulnerability and taunted her for her barrenness.

Elkanah tried to comfort his beloved wife. He once asked, "Why do you feel so bad? Don't I mean more to you than ten sons?" (1 Samuel 1:8).

Hannah took her pain to the house of the Lord, the tabernacle in Shiloh. There she unloaded her burdens. She wept. She prayed. She made a vow to give her firstborn son back to God for a lifetime of service, if only he would allow her to get pregnant. When her voice faltered, she silently mouthed the desires of her soul.

Eli, the priest, interrupted her prayer time. "How long are you going to stay drunk?" He demanded, "Sober up!" (1 Samuel 1:14).

A less committed woman would have mistaken his words for the last straw—or perhaps the final outrage. For her to pour her heart out to God only to be accused of public drunkenness by his priest hardly seems fair.

Yet Hannah was not dissuaded. She pleaded her case to the priest, who was moved by her anguish and sorrow. Eli reassured her, "Go home. Everything will be fine. The God of Israel will answer your prayer" (1 Samuel 1:17).

Hannah soon became pregnant and gave birth to Samuel. After she weaned her son, Hannah took him back to the tabernacle in Shiloh and left him with Eli. Following through with her vow, she gave him over to a lifetime in God's service. Before leaving Shiloh, Hannah prayed a joyous song of praise (see 1 Samuel 2:1–10). Imagine the mixture of pride, joy, relief, vindication, and thankfulness she must have felt as she watched Samuel become a revered prophet, priest, and leader of Israel.

Hannah refused to give up praying for a son, even when things seemed hopeless. Some may chalk that up to stubbornness or obsession. She continued to pray and trust God. Perhaps the reason she kept praying for a son is that God never told her to stop.

And if that's the case, we can learn a lot from Hannah's example.

*Life Lesson: If you sense that something is God's will for your life, don't let go. Don't get discouraged. Don't stop praying.*

1 Samuel 1:9–11 *When the sacrifice had been offered, and they had eaten the meal, Hannah got up and went to pray. Eli was sitting in his chair near the door to the place of worship. Hannah was heartbroken and was crying as she prayed, "LORD All-Powerful, I am your servant, but I am so miserable! Please let me have a son. I promise to give him to you for as long as he lives, and his hair will never be cut."*

For more on Hannah, read 1 Samuel 1.

I PRAISE YOU, LORD,

FOR ANSWERING MY PRAYERS.

YOU ARE MY STRONG SHIELD,

AND I TRUST YOU COMPLETELY.

YOU HAVE HELPED ME,

AND I WILL CELEBRATE

AND THANK YOU IN SONG.

PSALM 28:6-7

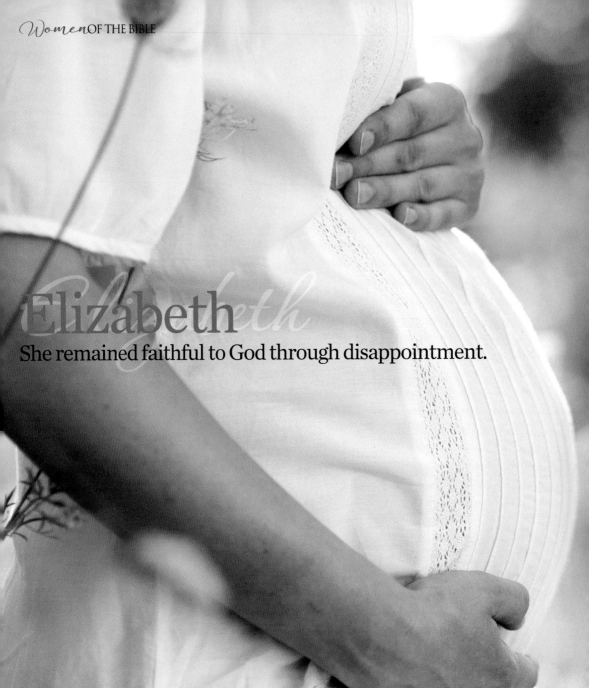

# Elizabeth

## She remained faithful to God through disappointment.

Elizabeth surely had heard her share of temple stories. She was descended from Aaron, the high priest. Her family history was chock-full of religious leaders. Her husband, Zechariah, served as a priest in the temple of Jerusalem. Imagine how often he brought his work home with him.

Despite her familiarity with the comings and goings of the temple, nothing could have prepared Elizabeth for the message Zechariah brought home one day. To be accurate, it's not what Zechariah said that stopped Elizabeth in her tracks.

It's what he didn't say.

The message was so fantastic and so far-fetched that Zechariah questioned it himself, even though it had been delivered by the angel Gabriel. Zechariah's unbelief cost him. The Lord temporarily took away his ability to speak.

So Zechariah had to use pantomime or the written word to tell Elizabeth, a woman well into her years, that she was going to give birth to a son.

And not just any son. He would be the forerunner of the Messiah, the one who would prepare Israel for the coming of the Savior.

If anyone else had intimated such a thing, Elizabeth might have taken it as a cruel joke. Her inability to bear children had been a source of disappointment and shame her entire adult life.

Yet she would be disgraced no more. Instead, she would be known as the mother of John the Baptist.

Why would God choose such an unlikely candidate for such an awesome privilege?

Perhaps the answer can be found in the following description, straight from God's Word:

*[Zechariah and Elizabeth] were good people and pleased the Lord God by obeying all that he had commanded. But they did not have children. Elizabeth could not have any, and both Zechariah and Elizabeth were already old.* (Luke 1:6–7)

Elizabeth refused to allow her disappointment to color her relationship with God. She and Zechariah remained faithful and obedient to him. Her circumstances did not affect her commitment.

Elizabeth was very old. As far as she knew, her prayers for a child had gone unanswered *permanently*. Yet she remained righteous in God's eyes. And God rewarded her beyond anything she could have imagined.

For that reason, Elizabeth is an ideal role model for anyone who's struggling with disappointment or disillusionment.

*Life Lesson:* **When you experience suffering and disappointment, remember that suffering produces endurance, which "builds character"; and character produces "a hope that will never disappoint" you** (Romans 5:3–5).

*Luke 1:57–64 When Elizabeth's son was born, her neighbors and relatives heard how kind the Lord had been to her, and they too were glad.*

*Eight days later they did for the child what the Law of Moses commands. They were going to name him Zechariah, after his father. But Elizabeth said, "No! His name is John."*

*The people argued, "No one in your family has ever been named John." So they motioned to Zechariah to find out what he wanted to name his son.*

*Zechariah asked for a writing tablet. Then he wrote, "His name is John." Everyone was amazed. Right away, Zechariah started speaking and praising God.*

For more on Elizabeth, read Luke 1.

# Salome, the Wife of Zebedee

## She learned that true greatness is found in servanthood, not status.

Such good boys, James and John. Handpicked by Jesus himself to serve as his disciples, they (along with Simon Peter) became something more. They became Jesus' confidantes and closest earthly companions.

A mother can be forgiven her pride, can't she? And what's a little ambition among friends? Was it such a leap to imagine her sons being given favored status in Jesus' eternal reign?

How hopeful Salome must have been when she made her request of Jesus: "When you come into your kingdom, please let one of my sons sit at your right side and the other at your left" (Matthew 20:21).

How stunned she must have been by his response: "You know foreign rulers like to order their people around. And their great leaders have full power over everyone they rule. But don't act like them. If you want to be great, you must be the servant of all the others. And if you want to be first, you must be the slave of the rest" (Matthew 20:25–27).

If Salome was disappointed by his answer, she shouldn't have been. She and Jesus were on the same page. They both wanted greatness for James and John. The only difference was that Jesus knew how they could achieve it. He knew that real greatness is found in servanthood.

Personal status and places of honor are illusions of greatness. They're what people with limited imaginations believe greatness involves. True greatness, Jesus pointed out, involves laying aside the useless props of pomp and glory and embracing the role of servant. He held himself up as an example. No one was greater than he because no one was a greater servant than he.

Salome apparently took Jesus' words to heart. Sometime later, she followed Jesus to Golgotha in order to be there for him during his crucifixion. And she was on her way to prepare his body for burial when she learned of his resurrection. Those are the actions of a servant. Those are the actions of a great woman.

*Zebedee's Wife* (1072–1078). Basilica Sant'Angelo. Formis, Italy.

*Life Lesson: If you devote yourself to serving others, you will discover what it means to be respected and honored.*

## A Contrast in Names

Salome's name comes from the Aramaic word *shalom*, which means "peace." Interestingly, her sons were known for their spirited temperaments (see Mark 9:38; Luke 9:54). Jesus gave them the nickname *Boanerges*, meaning "Thunderbolts" (Mark 3:17). Could it be that this peaceful-loving mother accompanied her boys as they followed Jesus in order to keep their thunderous behavior in check?

### Matthew 20:20–28

*The mother of James and John came to Jesus with her two sons. She knelt down and started begging him to do something for her. Jesus asked her what she wanted, and she said, "When you come into your kingdom, please let one of my sons sit at your right side and the other at your left." Jesus answered, "Not one of you knows what you are asking. Are you able to drink from the cup that I must soon drink from?" James and John said, "Yes, we are!" Jesus replied, "You certainly will drink from my cup! But it isn't for me to say who will sit at my right side and at my left. This is for my Father to say." When the ten other disciples heard this, they were angry with the two brothers. But Jesus called the disciples together and said: "You know that foreign rulers like to order their people around. And their great leaders have full power over everyone they rule. But don't act like them. If you want to be great, you must be the servant of all the others. And if you want to be first, you must be the slave of the rest. The Son of Man did not come to be a slave master, but a slave who will give his life to rescue many people."*

# THE WICKED:
## Four Women Who Embraced Evil

Not everyone in the Bible who encountered God or his people came away from the experience a changed person. Some may not have recognized their need to change. Others may have been too mired in guilt to believe that change was possible.

A select few, however, seemed to revel in their estrangement from God. In fact, they actively opposed him. They ignored his commands. They pursued other gods—and persuaded good people to follow suit. They sought to harm God's representatives. They abused their power and position. They embraced wickedness. They plumbed the depths of evil.

These are the villainous women of Scripture, the notorious characters whose depravity stands in stark contrast to the righteousness God calls his people to. Though they bedeviled the faithful at every turn, these wicked women also served as important cautionary figures.

Suffice it to say, their wickedness did not go unpunished. Sometimes that punishment was severe. And when God's people saw what happened to those who strayed from his will, they were inspired to draw closer to him.

# chapter 8

In this chapter, we'll look at four women who definitely qualify as villains:

- The medium of Endor, whose dark sorcery was no match for God's power
- Jezebel, who led Israel into all kinds of wickedness and idolatry
- Athaliah, whose lust for power drove her to slaughter most of her heirs
- Herodias, who orchestrated the beheading of John the Baptist because he dared to speak against her illicit marriage

# The Medium of Endor

## In the midst of her darkness, she encountered the power of God.

For more on the medium of Endor, read 1 Samuel 28.

**1 Samuel 28:7–11** *Then Saul told his officers, "Find me a woman who can talk to the spirits of the dead. I'll go to her and find out what's going to happen." His servants told him, "There's a woman at Endor who can talk to spirits of the dead." That night, Saul put on different clothing so nobody would recognize him. Then he and two of his men went to the woman, and asked, "Will you bring up the ghost of someone for us?" The woman said, "Why are you trying to trick me and get me killed? You know King Saul has killed everyone who talks to the spirits of the dead!" Saul replied, "I swear by the living* LORD *that nothing will happen to you because of this." "Who do you want me to bring up?" she asked. "Bring up the ghost of Samuel," he answered.*

The woman's heart must have raced a little as she watched three men approach her home. Times were hard for a witch. Thanks to King Saul's decree that all mediums be banished from Israel, it was open season on practitioners of the dark arts. Now every visit meant possible arrest.

When one of the men said he needed to speak to someone who had died, alarm bells must have sounded in her head.

"Why are you trying to trick me and get me killed"? the woman demanded. "You know King Saul has killed everyone who talks to the spirits of the dead!" (1 Samuel 28:9).

The man swore an oath in God's name (now there's irony for you) that nothing bad would happen to her. Then he asked to see Samuel, the beloved prophet and priest who had recently died.

The woman called for Samuel—and then screamed when he appeared. It wasn't the apparition that scared her, though. The medium suddenly recognized the man sitting across from her: King Saul.

This wasn't a trick, though. The king was desperate to talk to Samuel—desperate to receive a message from his God. The message Samuel gave him, however, only increased the king's despair.

According to the deceased prophet, God had taken the kingdom from Saul and given it to Saul's rival, David. The mighty Philistine army would be the Lord's instrument of judgment. Saul's forces faced certain defeat. Saul and his sons faced certain death.

The certainty of Samuel's words proved too much for Saul, who fell to the ground, paralyzed with fear. The medium, no longer fearing for her life, urged him to eat. She prepared some meat and unleavened bread. She fed Saul and his men and sent them on their way.

That's where the Bible narrative concerning the medium of Endor ends. As far as we know, her life may have continued for some time. But what direction did her life take?

Is it too optimistic to believe she came away from the encounter a changed woman? She had, after all, been used by the God of Israel. She also saw every event foretold by Samuel come to fruition. Perhaps the experience had a lasting impact on her. Perhaps she sensed a new future.

*Life Lesson: God can use you to accomplish amazing things through his power, even when life may seem dark or your circumstances discouraging.*

## Disgusting Practices

Practices of divination and sorcery were common among the people of Canaan. God strictly prohibited his people from engaging in such practices. Before they entered the promised land, Moses warned, "Don't sacrifice your son or daughter. And don't try to use any kind of magic or witchcraft to tell fortunes or to cast spells or to talk with spirits of the dead. The LORD is disgusted with anyone who does these things" (Deuteronomy 18:10–12a).

# Jezebel

## She promoted idol worship in Israel.

### Following in Her Father's Footsteps

Jezebel's father reigned for thirty-two years as king of Tyre and Sidon and also served as a priest of the Canaanite goddess Asherah. His name, *Ethbaal*, means "Baal is with him." It is no wonder his devoted daughter worked so hard to spread the worship of the Canaanite gods throughout her husband's kingdom.

If your name is still used as a synonym for a wicked, shameless woman *more than 2,500 years after your death*, it's safe to say you were no mere amateur when it came to transgressive behavior. So it was with Jezebel.

Privileged from birth, Jezebel was the daughter of Ethbaal, the king of Tyre (Phoenicia). As a young woman, she married Ahab, the king of Israel. The newly minted queen helped initiate a seismic shift in the nation's religious landscape. A devout Baalist, Jezebel was effectively put in charge of Israel's domestic and religious affairs by her husband, who had an affinity for the Baal religion.

Jezebel carried out her responsibilities with zeal. Her first order of business was to weaken the influence of the prevailing Yahweh religion. With the king's blessing, she led a persecution of the prophets of God, killing some and sending the rest into hiding, until only Elijah remained. She brought in 850 prophets of Baal and Asherah to replace them. When Elijah exposed her prophets as impotent frauds and turned the Israelites against them, Jezebel vowed to have him killed.

Jezebel was thoroughly seduced by the dark side of political power. Once a man named Naboth refused to sell his vineyard to the king. Jezebel arranged to have him falsely accused of blasphemy and stoned to death. Thus Ahab got his vineyard.

Such corruption requires a suitable punishment, and God did not disappoint. After King Ahab was killed in battle, an army commander named Jehu was given the task of destroying the king's descendants—as well as his notorious widow.

Jezebel was preparing for Jehu's arrival when her own servants grabbed her and threw her from a window to her death. Before Jezebel's body could be given a proper burial, it was eaten by stray dogs.

A wretched end to a wretched life.

What is the proper response to such amoral allegiance—to the type of destructive behavior Jezebel unleashed on Israel at the behest of her husband and king? For that answer, we need look no further than Elijah's example. First, we must oppose evil actions at every turn. We must speak out and take a public stand, regardless of the consequences.

In the end, though, we must leave vengeance in God's hands. He will deal with the perpetrators—in his own perfect time and his own perfect way.

*Life Lesson: Evil's season is short; God's righteousness will prevail—and with it, his judgment.*

2 Kings 9:30–37 *Jehu headed toward Jezreel, and when Jezebel heard he was coming, she put on eye shadow and brushed her hair. Then she stood at the window, waiting for him to arrive. As he walked through the city gate, she shouted down to him, "Why did you come here, you murderer? To kill the king? You're no better than Zimri!"*

*He looked up toward the window and asked, "Is anyone up there on my side?" A few palace workers stuck their heads out of a window, and Jehu shouted, "Throw her out the window!" They threw her down, and her blood splattered on the walls and on the horses that trampled her body.*

*Jehu left to get something to eat and drink. Then he told some workers, "Even though she was evil, she was a king's daughter, so make sure she has a proper burial."*

*But when they went out to bury her body, they found only her skull, her hands, and her feet. They reported this to Jehu, and he said, "The Lord told Elijah the prophet that Jezebel's body would be eaten by dogs right here in Jezreel. And he warned that her bones would be spread all over the ground like manure, so that no one could tell who it was."*

For more on Jezebel, read 1 Kings 18; 21; 2 Kings 9.

*The lifestyle of good people is like sunlight at dawn*
*that keeps getting brighter until broad daylight.*
*The lifestyle of the wicked is like total darkness,*
*and they will never know what makes them stumble.*
*Proverbs 4:18–19*

# Athaliah

Her desire for power led her to commit the unthinkable.

Is evil a genetic trait or a learned behavior?

We're not talking about your everyday sinful nature here. We're talking about an overwhelming bent toward wickedness—the kind of narcissistic, sociopathic behavior that destroys lives. Is this something a person is born with? Or is it something that is learned?

In the case of Athaliah, the answer to both questions is most likely yes.

As evil pedigrees go, Athaliah's is hard to top. Her father was King Ahab, perhaps the wickedest ruler in Israel's history. Whether her mother was the evil Queen Jezebel or another wife of Ahab is up for debate. Either way, there were some sinister genetics at work.

Athaliah's early years were promising, at least from a historical standpoint. She married King Jehoram of Judah, and that may be where Athaliah's problems intensified.

When Jehoram was killed, Athaliah's son Ahaziah inherited the throne. Many Bible scholars have suggested that Athaliah held on to her royal position by becoming one of her son's most trusted advisors—perhaps the true power behind the throne.

When Ahaziah died, though, it looked like Athaliah's reign would come to an end. That's when desperation set in. Realizing her only hope for holding on to power was to eliminate the competition, Athaliah launched a royal bloodbath. She ordered the executions of everyone with a legitimate claim to the throne—namely, her own grandchildren.

She got all but one. A grandson named Joash was hidden away in the temple until he was old enough to assume the throne. So Athaliah reigned as Israel's monarch for six years.

Her tenure was interrupted by Joash's reemergence. The people of Israel rallied around the rightful king. When Athaliah tried to quash their rebellion, they executed her.

Today Athaliah is remembered as one of Scripture's most extreme examples of the corrupting nature of power.

*Life Lesson: If you're not vigilant in maintaining a humble spirit and a God-honoring perspective, even a small taste of power—whether it's a promotion at work or an appointment to a position of authority—may be your spiritual undoing.*

**2 Kings 11:1–3** *As soon as Athaliah heard that her son King Ahaziah was dead, she decided to kill any relative who could possibly become king. She would have done that, but Jehosheba rescued Joash son of Ahaziah just as he was about to be murdered. Jehosheba, who was Jehoram's daughter and Ahaziah's half sister, hid her nephew Joash and his personal servant in a bedroom in the LORD's temple where he was safe from Athaliah. Joash hid in the temple with Jehosheba for six years while Athaliah ruled as queen of Judah.*

For more on Athaliah, read 2 Kings 11.

# Herodias

## She responded to criticism with bitterness and hatred.

A Jewish man publicly condemning a member of the Roman royal family? Where did he get the nerve, this John the so-called Baptist?

Who cares if it was wrong for her to divorce one heir to the throne and marry his half brother? That wasn't the point. No half-crazed prophet from the wilderness had any business commenting on her private life, let alone drumming up public opposition to it.

And Herodias was not a woman to cross.

Eventually, she exacted her revenge. When her second husband, Herod Antipas, threw a great party, Herodias arranged for her daughter to dance for the guests. Antipas was so pleased by her dance that he offered to grant her any request. Coached by her mother, the young dancer asked for the head of John the Baptist. Antipas had no choice but to comply, even though he personally liked John. To go back on his word in front of his guests would have been unthinkable. So Antipas ordered the beheading of John the Baptist.

What goes around comes around, of course. God wasn't about to let the murder of his prophet go unpunished. When the Roman emperor Caligula assumed power, Herodias was banished to Gaul, where she spent the rest of her life in exile, presumably (and impotently) plotting revenge against everyone else who had wronged her.

How might this story have turned out differently if Herodias had been more receptive to prophetic criticism?

Everyone is imperfect; few of us like to be reminded of this fact. Confrontation stings, at least initially. But if the criticism is valid, few things are more valuable.

*Life Lesson:* **Be willing to listen to criticism. Some of your most important growth may be prompted by the confrontation of someone who cares.**

**Mark 6:19–24** *Herodias had a grudge against John and wanted to kill him. But she could not do it because Herod was afraid of John and protected him. He knew that John was a good and holy man. Even though Herod was confused by what John said, he was glad to listen to him. And he often did.*

*Finally, Herodias got her chance when Herod gave a great birthday celebration for himself and invited his officials, his army officers, and the leaders of Galilee. The daughter of Herodias came in and danced for Herod and his guests. She pleased them so much that Herod said, "Ask for anything, and it's yours! I swear that I will give you as much as half of my kingdom, if you want it."*

*The girl left and asked her mother, "What do you think I should ask for?"*

*Her mother answered, "The head of John the Baptist!"*

## A Family Affair

John the Baptist had good reason to condemn Herodias's marriage to Herod Antipas. Old Testament law clearly forbade marriage between a man and his sister-in-law (see Leviticus 18:16; 20:21). Grounds for marriage were only acceptable if the man's brother had died without producing an heir.

# HAUNTED LIVES:
## Seven Women, the Choices They Made, and the Prices They Paid

The women of the Bible are a diverse lot. Their backgrounds and experiences are remarkably varied. Each story is unique, yet a common thread weaves its way through almost every account.

In many cases, these women discovered that one decision—one fateful choice—made at a crucial moment can reverberate for a lifetime.

chapter 9

Making a wise choice under such circumstances— that is, choosing to follow God's will even when it's difficult to do so—places one in the pantheon of Bible heroes, the giants of the faith. What's more, making a wise decision at the right moment can have several unexpected results:

- Opening doors that weren't accessible before
- Revealing previously untapped inner strength
- Casting a person in a different light in other people's eyes
- Improving one's quality of life
- Leading someone to play a pivotal role in God's plan

Other women in the Bible could attest to the fact that unwise choices made at crucial moments can also set the tone for the rest of one's life. These women faced a crucible and failed. Some impetuously made the wrong call. Others allowed circumstances to overwhelm them. Some got caught up in a moment.

Their stories serve notice to everyone who seeks to follow God. We must stay vigilant and make choices that honor him. The stakes are too high to choose unwisely.

In this chapter, we'll look at seven women who had to come to terms with decisions they made:

- Lot's wife, who couldn't leave behind her old life
- Lot's daughters, who chose to take matters into their own hands instead of trusting God to provide for their needs
- Delilah, who betrayed Samson for her own personal gain
- Maacah, who used her position as the queen mother to promote idolatry in Israel
- Gomer, who cheated on her husband repeatedly
- Sapphira, who pretended to give a certain sum to the Lord's work while withholding some of it for herself

# Lot's Wife

## She couldn't leave the past behind.

The escape from Sodom was more than just a lifesaving intervention; it was a chance for a fresh start.

The angelic visitors, messengers from God, offered Lot and his family a way out of their notoriously evil hometown. These visitors seemed unafraid of the dangers lurking in Sodom—even as crowds of people gathered outside Lot's door, demanding to have their way with the men. Perhaps it was that fearlessness that convinced Lot and his family to believe the visitors' message. Obviously the power they represented was greater than all the evil in Sodom.

That power—God himself—was preparing to unleash utter destruction on the city and anyone who remained in it. The visitors' instructions to Lot's family were urgent: run and don't look back.

Don't. Look. Back.

God, in his goodness, had delivered Lot and his family from their old lives. He'd given them an escape route from all the wickedness that surrounded them. He'd selected a new destination for them. He'd offered them a chance to start again.

Everything good in their lives lay in front of them. All God asked was that they keep their attention fixed on the path he had laid out for them. He wanted them to make a complete break from their old lives.

What compelled Lot's wife to turn around? Was her life in Sodom too ingrained for her to walk away? What friendships did she leave behind? Did she feel the pangs of nostalgia for the "good old days"? Did she prefer the devil she knew to the God she didn't? Did she doubt the Lord's compassion or his ability to make something good of their lives post-Sodom?

Whatever the case, God recognized the intent of her heart. The moment her gaze fixed on the burning ruins of Sodom, he sapped the life force from her body, leaving nothing but a pillar of salt—as swift a death sentence as you'll find anywhere in Scripture. Her life ended before it could begin again, all because she could not leave her past behind.

We all have complicated relationships with our checkered pasts. The more sordid our past, the more complicated our relationship with it. Yet God provides the means that not only allows us to move beyond our past failures but actually compels us to do so. God cannot rescue someone who clings to the "good old days" and doesn't realize how much the past pales in comparison to the future he offers.

*Life Lesson: The ability to leave your past behind is essential to enjoying God's fulfilling future.*

For more on Lot's wife, read Genesis 19.

## Where in the World?

It is believed that Sodom, one of the "cities of the valley" (Genesis 19:29), was located somewhere south and east of the Dead Sea, a body of water that cannot support aquatic life because of its unusually high salt levels. Salt formations still exist today in the region and serve as reminders of Lot's wife's fateful last glance toward wicked Sodom.

*Destruction of Sodom and Gomorrah*, Gustave Doré (1832–1883)

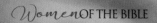

These little troubles are getting us ready for an
eternal glory that will make all our troubles seem
like nothing. Things that are seen don't last
forever, but things that are not seen are eternal.
That is why we keep our minds on the things
that cannot be seen.

2 Corinthians 4:17–18

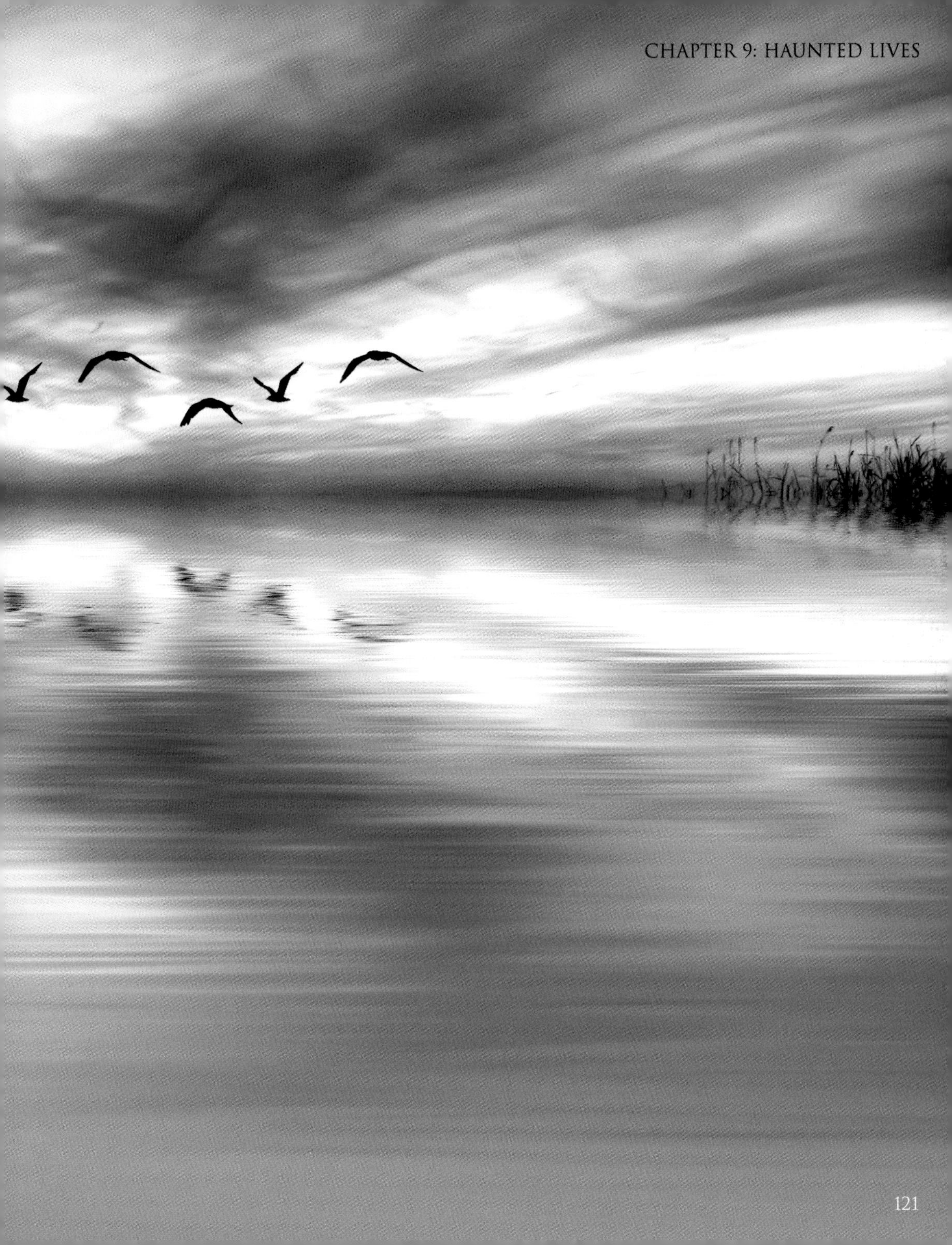

# Lot's Daughters

## Their choices reflected their inability to trust God.

If we're assigning blame, let's start with the patriarch. Lot made a purposeful decision to move his family to Sodom—hardly the best place to raise a family. He selected fiancés for his daughters from among the city's inhabitants.

Lot's daughters spent years in that wretched place, where oppression was the norm and morality was but a distant memory. The Bible suggests that Lot and his family may have tried to distance themselves from the more blatantly wicked elements in the city, but it was little use. The influences of Sodom surrounded them. Lot unhesitatingly offered his virgin daughters to appease a sexually violent crowd in order to spare the lives of two visitors to his home.

Like their mother, Lot's daughters must have been conflicted when the mysterious visitors told the family to leave Sodom before it was destroyed by God. On the one hand, practically everyone they knew—including their fiancés, who refused to leave—lived in Sodom. On the other hand, if God himself sends someone to rescue you, it's safe to assume he has other plans for your life.

Perhaps it was the prospect of those plans coming to pass that kept their eyes fixed ahead, even when their mother looked back and lost her life. That forward thinking, however, only lasted so long.

Sometime later, Lot's daughters were living in a cave with their father when they realized that every eligible bachelor in the region had been incinerated. That left only one man (as far as they could see) to father their own children.

*Father* being the operative word.

One night, Lot's daughters got him drunk. Without his realizing it, his older daughter slept with him and became pregnant. The next night, they did the same thing and the younger daughter became pregnant.

Perhaps Lot's daughters were so blinded by the loss of everything they knew that they could not imagine what future God might have for them. They looked to themselves and not God for the answer.

Where will you look for help when crisis comes?

*Life Lesson:* **The best way to ensure that you make God-honoring choices is to surround yourself with godly influences and trust God for his provision.**

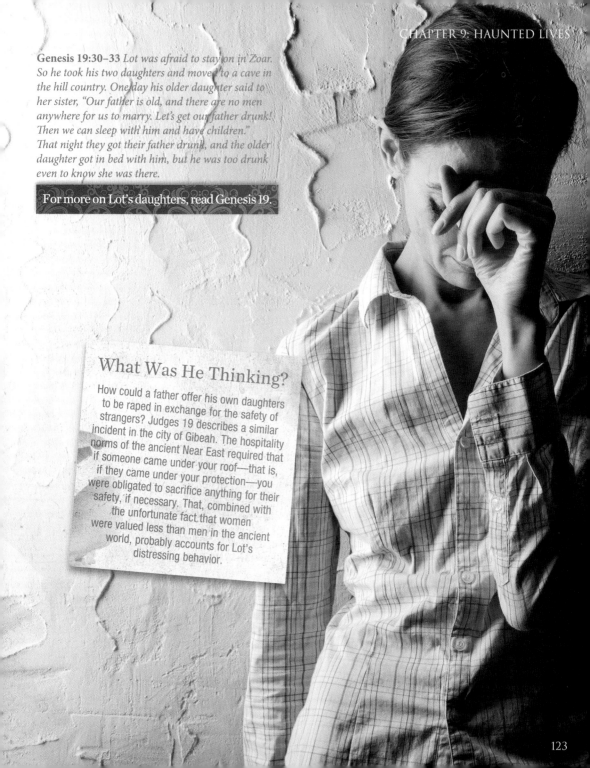

**Genesis 19:30–33** *Lot was afraid to stay on in Zoar. So he took his two daughters and moved to a cave in the hill country. One day his older daughter said to her sister, "Our father is old, and there are no men anywhere for us to marry. Let's get our father drunk! Then we can sleep with him and have children." That night they got their father drunk, and the older daughter got in bed with him, but he was too drunk even to know she was there.*

For more on Lot's daughters, read Genesis 19.

## What Was He Thinking?

How could a father offer his own daughters to be raped in exchange for the safety of strangers? Judges 19 describes a similar incident in the city of Gibeah. The hospitality norms of the ancient Near East required that if someone came under your roof—that is, if they came under your protection—you were obligated to sacrifice anything for their safety, if necessary. That, combined with the unfortunate fact that women were valued less than men in the ancient world, probably accounts for Lot's distressing behavior.

# Delilah

## She misused a man's heart for personal gain.

For more on Delilah, read Judges 16.

*Judges 16:15–18 "Samson," Delilah said, "you claim to love me, but you don't mean it! You've made me look like a fool three times now, and you still haven't told me why you are so strong." Delilah started nagging and pestering him day after day, until he couldn't stand it any longer.*

*Finally, Samson told her the truth. "I have belonged to God ever since I was born, so my hair has never been cut. If it were ever cut off, my strength would leave me, and I would be as weak as anyone else."*

*Delilah realized that he was telling the truth. So she sent someone to tell the Philistine rulers, "Come to my house one more time. Samson has finally told me the truth."*

What could one woman do that the entire Philistine army could not? Subdue the strongest man who ever lived, that's what.

Samson, the Israelite judge blessed with enormous strength, had wreaked havoc on the Philistines for years. He had burned their grain fields and destroyed their vineyards and olive groves. He had killed 1,000 Philistine warriors at one time, armed with nothing but the jawbone of a donkey. He had torn out the city gates of Gaza.

Fortunately for the Philistines, Samson had a weakness. He loved Philistine women—especially a beautiful woman named Delilah. The poor sap fell hard for her, much to the delight of the Philistine rulers. Delilah, after all, could be bought for a price.

And what a price! Each ruler offered to give her 1,100 pieces of silver—more than enough for her to live comfortably for the rest of her life. All she had to do was uncover the secret to Samson's strength.

Delilah wasted no time—and very little subtlety. "Samson, what makes you so strong? How can I tie you up so you can't get away? Come on, you can tell me" (Judges 16:6). Such a request might have raised suspicions in most people, but Samson had little in common with most people.

The love-struck strongman told Delilah that if he were tied up with seven new bowstrings, he would become as weak as anyone else. Then he fell asleep. When he awoke, he was tied up with seven new bowstrings, and a group of Philistines were coming to get him.

Samson broke the strings like thread, much to Delilah's anger. He had lied to her. Twice more she asked him the secret of his strength. Twice more he gave her false answers. Twice more a group of Philistines came to get him, only to be scared away by a still-strong Samson.

By the fourth time, Samson should have known what Delilah was up to. Yet such was her hold over him that she finally managed to coax a truthful answer from him. Samson revealed that if someone cut his hair, he would become as weak as any other man.

Before you could say, "A little off the top, please," Samson's hair was shorn, his eyes were gouged out, and he was taken prisoner and forced to grind grain for the Philistines.

Delilah took her blood money, which is where her part in the biblical narrative ends.

Did she ever see Samson again? Did she feel pity for him or guilt for herself? Was she among the thousands present at the temple of Dagon during the festival in honor of the Philistine

### A Hefty Price

Disarming Samson resulted in no small prize for Delilah. The amount of silver the Philistine rulers paid her— 1,100 pieces or 140 pounds—was equal to the price of about 275 slaves. (Source: The NIV Study Bible)

god? Did she recoil when officials brought out the blind and presumably helpless Samson to endure the taunts of the crowd? Did she notice—too late—as Samson placed his hands on the load-bearing pillars that his hair had grown back? The Bible says Samson died, along with over 3,000 Philistines, when his renewed strength caused the collapse of the temple. Yet he was as good as dead the moment he laid his head on Delilah's lap. To quote the final line of *King Kong*: "'Twas beauty killed the beast."

If you're the object of someone's affection, you have access to that person's heart. Regardless of how you feel about that person, you have a God-given responsibility to handle their heart with care—just as you want your heart to be handled.

*Life Lesson:* **If someone gives you their heart, treat it with respect and kindness.**

# Maacah

## She hastened the downfall of her kingdom.

As surely as Jesus' arrival divided history in two—into BC and AD—the lives of those he encountered were also divided in two. In most cases, life after an encounter with Jesus bore very little resemblance to life before it.

chapter 11

Such was the transforming power of Jesus.

For some people, the changes were physical and miraculous. Lifelong disabilities, illnesses, and afflictions were cured with a simple word or touch from the Lord. Loved ones were restored to health. Families were healed.

For others, the changes were emotional. People whose lives had been wrecked by isolation, poor choices, or self-loathing discovered what it means to be accepted, forgiven, made clean, and given a fresh start.

For some, the changes were directional. People whose lives had seemed aimless or unimportant were given a vital purpose. Those who wielded very little power or authority in their communities were assigned positions of influence in Jesus' ministry.

In this chapter, we'll look at nine women whose lives were changed forever by their encounters with Jesus:

- The Syrophoenician woman, whose dogged pursuit of healing for her demon-possessed daughter moved Jesus to help her
- The woman with an illness, who correctly believed a simple touch of Jesus' garment would be sufficient to heal her
- Mary, witness to the crucifixion, whose faithfulness and commitment to Jesus did not end with his death
- Martha, whose priorities were rearranged by Jesus himself
- Mary of Bethany, whose single-minded devotion to the Lord served her well
- Joanna, who used her power and influence to support Jesus' ministry
- The Samaritan woman, who accepted Jesus' offer of "living water"
- The woman caught in adultery, whose life was spared and redirected, thanks to Jesus' intervention
- Mary Magdalene, who experienced redemption and then gave her life to her Redeemer

Their experiences give hope to anyone who
- suffers from a debilitating affliction or injury;
- struggles with guilt, shame, or self-worth issues;
- feels limited or unfulfilled by present circumstances; or
- believes they could make a difference, if only things were different.

# The Syrophoenician Woman

Her faith, humility, and persistence moved Jesus' heart.

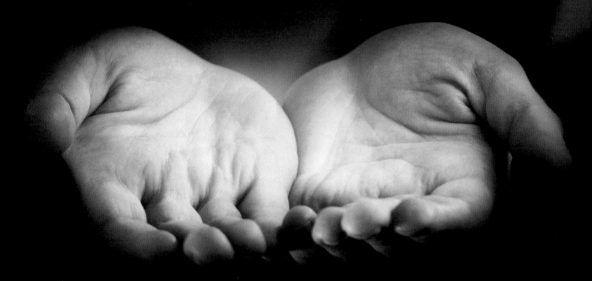

For more on the Syrophoenician Woman,
read Matthew 15.

Jesus' behavior in Matthew 15 seems callous, even offensive, to our modern sensibilities. Yet the woman on the receiving end appears to have been anything but offended.

At first, Jesus ignored the woman's request: "Have pity on me! My daughter is full of demons" (Matthew 15:22). His silence and the woman's persistence were so disquieting that Jesus' disciples urged him to send the woman away.

But the woman would not be deterred, even after Jesus replied that his first priority was to help the "lost sheep" of Israel—and that for him to assist a Gentile (a non-Jew) would be taking children's food and tossing it to the dogs.

The question is, why did the Syrophoenician woman put up with such treatment?

Could it be that she expected rejection and was braced for such a response? After all, Jesus was a respected Jewish teacher and miracle worker, and she was a Gentile woman. She'd likely been called a dog by Jewish people enough times in her life to know where she stood in their pecking order. In desperation, she may have hoped that if she allowed herself to be debased long enough, Jesus eventually might take pity on her and help her daughter.

Or could it be that this Gentile woman understood Jesus even better than even his followers did? Perhaps she recognized a kindness in his eyes or a playfulness in his voice that belied his words. Perhaps she sensed that he was making a point to his followers and that he really intended to help her.

That might explain how she was able to maintain her humble doggedness. To Jesus' dog comment, she replied, "Lord, this is true . . . but even puppies get the crumbs that fall from their owner's table" (Matthew 15:27).

If she was banking on the hope that Jesus would reward such humble tenacity, then she was not disappointed.

"Dear woman," Jesus said to her, "you really do have a lot of faith, and you will be given what you want" (Matthew 15:28). The woman's daughter was instantly healed.

There's a lesson or two in the Syrophoenician woman's experience for everyone who's ever taken a request to the Lord.

**Lesson one:** silence does not equal indifference. The fact that a prayer isn't answered immediately doesn't mean the Lord doesn't care about you.

**Lesson two:** a humble spirit combined with a healthy dose of persistence is a powerful combination, as far as God is concerned. To give up on a God-honoring prayer too early is to risk missing a miracle—or something close to it.

*Life Lesson:* **The fact that the Lord hasn't yet answered a prayer request yet is no indication that he won't answer it in the future.**

The Syrophoenician woman lived near the pagan cities of Tyre and Sidon in Phoenicia, northwest of Galilee. Matthew described her as a "Canaanite" (Matthew 15:22), a term that is only used once in the New Testament. By describing the woman as a Canaanite, Matthew made it clear to his readers that she was a Gentile, not a Jew, and that Jesus' offer of grace extends to all people.

For more on the Woman with an Illness, read Mark 5.

## The Outcast

This woman had suffered more than just a physical ailment for years. She had endured being ostracized, shunned, ignored, avoided, and left alone. Her condition rendered her unclean, according to the laws of the Old Testament, and anyone she touched would have had to wash their clothes and bathe their bodies (see Leviticus 15:19–23). Even the smallest touch from this diseased woman would have been repulsive to most people. But Jesus wasn't most people.

# The Woman with an Illness

She placed her hope in the only One who could heal her.

For twelve long years the woman had sought treatment for her constant bleeding. She'd spent all her money on doctors. She'd endured more painful procedures and would-be cures than she could count. Nothing had worked.

She'd exhausted every option. She had nowhere else to turn, except to the teacher from Galilee. The one with the healing powers. The one people had been talking about.

Surely the woman was a bit skeptical when she first heard the stories. What could this teacher do that all the doctors in the region couldn't?

But hope dies hard. So when this teacher, this Jesus of Nazareth, passed through her village, she went to see him. As did nearly everyone else from the surrounding area.

The size of the crowd made a face-to-face encounter with Jesus nearly impossible. Even from a distance, though, the woman must have sensed that he could help her. Something inside her recognized something inside him. She pressed through the melee, hoping to get within arm's reach of the man.

She didn't need his undivided attention. After all, who was she to ask for a personal audience with him? She didn't need the touch of his hand or even the healing command of his voice. She could sense his power, his ability to make her whole. All she needed was a moment's connection to him. She was certain of it.

So as Jesus passed by a few feet in front of her, the woman reached out in faith and touched his robe. At that moment Jesus felt power go out from him. Immediately the disease left her body. She was healed!

Jesus turned to the crowd and asked, "Who touched my clothes?" (Mark 5:30). She was caught! Trembling, she fell to her knees and acknowledged what she'd done. But Jesus wasn't angry. He wanted to make sure she understood what had happened. He wanted her to know she was changed forever.

"You are now well because of your faith. May God give you peace! You are healed, and you will no longer be in pain" (Mark 5:34).

Every one of us has a pre-existing condition—a physical, emotional, relational, or spiritual affliction that affects our quality of life. In some cases, we may not fully understand the problem or where it came from or how deeply it's affecting us. We know only that we need *something.*

The woman in the story took her affliction to Jesus. She had no clue what he would do, only a gut feeling that he would do something. Her life changed forever as a result.

That same opportunity is available to us. If we take our affliction to Jesus, he may not heal us immediately, as he did with the woman. In fact, he may not physically heal us at all. But he will transform us spiritually. He'll give us perspective, hope, support, and strength to endure—and thrive.

*Life Lesson:* **If you hold fast to God's promises, you will be blessed.**

The LORD forgives our sins,

heals us when we are sick,

and protects us from death.

His kindness and love

are a crown on our heads.

Each day that we live,

he provides for our needs

and gives us the strength

of a young eagle.

PSALM
103:3–5

For more on Mary,
read Mark 15.

# Mary, Witness to the Crucifixion

## She cared enough to show up.

Crucifixion was the stuff of nightmares, a barbaric form of capital punishment carried out in public venues. No normal person could endure the spectacle of such horrific suffering without enduring emotional damage. After all, some things can't be unseen.

But that's precisely what Mary endured as a follower of Jesus who chose to be present at his crucifixion, despite the risks to her psyche and the very real danger of being connected to this rabble-rouser from Galilee.

The Bible doesn't offer insight into Mary's motivation. Perhaps she was there to support Jesus' mother. Perhaps as a follower of Jesus, Mary felt compelled to see his ministry through to its conclusion. Perhaps she was there to make sure his body received proper treatment for burial.

We do not know Mary's reason for being there, but the point is that she was there. If any comfort, support, or assistance was needed, she was on hand to provide it.

Who can say what her presence meant to Jesus? How much comfort did it give him to see the loving face of one of his closest followers? Did he look to her when the vitriol of his enemies became too much to bear? Did her presence ease his emotional anguish, even for a moment?

Mary was there when Jesus died. Though she might have wanted to be anywhere else at that moment, she was there. She made a difference because she was present.

Sometimes being present is the most caring gesture we can make for another person. We may not know the right thing to say or do. In fact, there may not be anything to say. But if we show up with a servant's heart and a desire to help, that's more than enough.

*Life Lesson: **If you care enough to show up—to be present in the lives of people in need—God will use you to make a difference.***

## Which Mary?

There are seven women by the name of Mary in the New Testament. This Mary was "the mother of the younger James and of Joseph" (Mark 15:40–41). She and several other women arrived at Jesus' empty tomb before anyone else and told the disciples the news of the resurrection (see Mark 16:1-8; Luke 24:1–12). Some scholars believe she was "the other Mary" mentioned in Matthew 28:1, who was Jesus' mother's sister and the wife of Clopas (see John 19:25).

For more on Martha, read Luke 10.

# Martha

## Her distractions clouded her need to deepen her relationship with Jesus.

Martha was a consummate host. When Jesus visited the home she shared with her sister, Mary, Martha was the one who made sure everything was just right. She busied herself preparing the meal and anticipating her guest's needs. Mary, on the other hand, simply sat at the Lord's feet, soaking up his every word.

Martha mistook her sister's action for laziness and complained to Jesus. The Lord gently reminded her of the value of Mary's choice.

"Martha, Martha! You are worried and upset about so many things, but only one thing is necessary. Mary has chosen what is best, and it will not be taken away from her" (Luke 10:41–42).

Martha got so caught up in the business of being a good host that she had no time to enjoy the invitation to become a disciple. Preparing a meal for the Messiah was certainly a worthy endeavor, but not if it came at the expense of sitting at his feet and learning from him.

Contained in Jesus' gentle reminder to Martha was an invitation to view herself in a different light. To sit at the feet of a Jewish teacher as her sister did was to assume the posture of a disciple. In Jesus' day, such an honor was reserved for men. It was rarely, if ever, bestowed on women. By refusing to dismiss Mary so she could help Martha, Jesus gave Martha a much greater gift: a place of welcome at his feet, as the equal of any man.

It's easy to get caught up in the "red tape" of daily living. Responsibilities that may seem pressing—resolving schedule conflicts, personality clashes, budgetary concerns, and the like—have a way of distracting us from the greatest gift of all: the invitation to become disciples of Jesus.

When we forget our place of welcome at Jesus' feet, we need his gentle reminder: "You are worried and upset about so many things, but only one thing is necessary."

If we focus first on that one thing—deepening our relationship with Jesus—we'll be better equipped to deal with secondary issues.

*Life Lesson:* **Jesus welcomes you to sit at his feet and become his disciple. Compared to that, everything else is secondary.**

## Martha's Faith

The treatment of Martha in Luke 10 focuses on her household distractions, yet she should be remembered for her faith and witness to Jesus. At the time of the death of her brother, Lazarus, Martha confessed that Jesus is the Messiah, the One her people had been waiting and hoping for (John 11:27).

# Mary of Bethany

## She focused her attention and devotion on her Savior.

Mary, the sister of Martha and Lazarus, is set apart in the New Testament by one remarkable skill. Call it extreme focus—the ability to devote her complete attention to a single task or person.

The first evidence of her skill is found in the story of Jesus' visit to the home Mary and Martha shared. While Martha busied herself with meal preparation and other hosting duties, Mary sat in rapt attention at the Lord's feet. For a few hours or more, Mary tuned out everything else in her life in order to focus on Jesus. (See Luke 10:38–42.)

Understandably, this caused some friction with Martha, who wanted Mary's help. But Mary seemed to understand the importance of spending one-on-one time with Jesus right then and there. She sensed that Jesus wouldn't deny her the opportunity to sit at his feet—to take the posture of a disciple—even though she was a woman living in a patriarchal society.

Martha may have been annoyed by Mary's choice under the circumstances, but Jesus was quite pleased by it. In fact, he encouraged it: "Only one thing is necessary. Mary has chosen what is best, and it will not be taken away from her" (Luke 10:42).

A similar event occurred near the end of Jesus' life. On his way to Jerusalem, Jesus and his disciples stopped at Lazarus's house, where they enjoyed the fellowship and hospitality of Lazarus, Martha, and Mary.

After dinner, Mary stunned her visitors by kneeling in front of Jesus, pouring a pint of pure nard—an extremely expensive perfume—on his feet, and wiping them with her hair. The cost of the perfume was equivalent to a year's salary for an average laborer, but Mary thought nothing of it. Her focus was the task at hand.

Judas Iscariot, the one who held the purse strings for the disciples, took her to task for wasting so much money. Mary made no reply. She was too intent on anointing Jesus.

So Jesus responded for her. "Leave her alone! She has kept this perfume for the day of my burial. You will always have the poor with you, but you won't always have me" (John 12:7–8).

At that moment, Mary knew she needed to focus everything on Jesus. She was right. We can learn much from her example.

Life goes by at an alarming rate. If we wait for it to slow down, we'll miss countless opportunities to spend time in Jesus' presence. Like Mary, we must seize our moments, regardless of the circumstances. Others may not understand, but Jesus does. And he rewards those who work to maintain an intimate relationship with him.

*Life Lesson:* **Regular sessions of extreme focus on Jesus and his work will do your soul good.**

For more on Mary of Bethany, read John 12.

## A Not-So-Simple Dinner Party

Perfume was customarily used during only the most joyous or the most sorrowful of occasions—festivals and burials. Mary's seemingly outrageous actions at a simple dinner party inadvertently pointed to Jesus' imminent death and burial.

For more on Joanna, read Luke 24.

# Joanna

## She cared enough to support the believers.

Joanna was a woman of means and influence. Her husband, Chuza, managed the household of Herod Antipas, the governor of Galilee. As the wife of a government official, Joanna enjoyed a certain measure of wealth and influence. And as a prominent member of Jewish society, she had no shortage of options for spending her time and resources (see Luke 8:1–3).

Joanna's "investment strategy" was shaped by a chance encounter with Jesus. The Lord had healed Joanna of an unnamed affliction—and thus changed the direction of her life. She became a devoted follower and avid supporter of Jesus and his ministry. She had a lot to give, personally and financially, and she gave it freely.

In investment terms, her outlook was bullish. Her portfolio was high-risk, high-yield. She was "all in" where Jesus was concerned, whether it involved her resources, her time, or her energies.

Joanna provided for Jesus and his disciples when they traveled. She made sure they were properly cared for. When Jesus moved his ministry from Galilee to Jerusalem, Joanna followed. In biblical times, it was unheard of and even scandalous for a woman to join the retinue of a traveling teacher. But Joanna clearly didn't care what others thought of her.

Her devotion was constant, even after Jesus was crucified. Joanna was one of the women who hurried to Jesus' tomb on the Sunday morning after his crucifixion to prepare his body for burial. She was among the first witnesses to the greatest news the world has ever received: "He has been raised from death" (Luke 24:6). She was one of the blessed few charged with carrying that news to Jesus' disciples and beyond.

The Christian landscape changed after Jesus ascended to heaven. The first-century church emerged as a force for discipleship and evangelism. The Roman Empire sought to limit the fledgling faith's influence by any means necessary.

Yet the return on Joanna's investment continued unabated. Her support and influence helped guide the church through a critical time in its development.

Joanna's choice to invest in Jesus and his ministry yielded dividends beyond anything she could have imagined. Her investment continues to produce returns today, because no conscientious believer can read Joanna's story without asking, How am I using my resources and influence for Christ's kingdom?

*Life Lesson:* **If you invest your time and resources in God-honoring ministry, you'll reap dividends in ways you can't even imagine.**

## The Same Joanna?

If, as some scholars think, the name Junia in Romans 16:7 is a variation of the name Joanna, the apostle Paul may have looked to Joanna as a spiritual leader in the church.

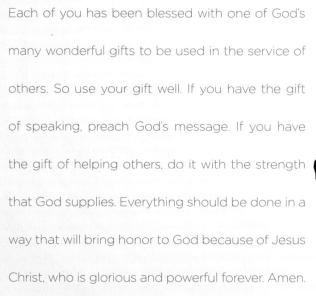

Each of you has been blessed with one of God's many wonderful gifts to be used in the service of others. So use your gift well. If you have the gift of speaking, preach God's message. If you have the gift of helping others, do it with the strength that God supplies. Everything should be done in a way that will bring honor to God because of Jesus Christ, who is glorious and powerful forever. Amen.

# gifts

1 Peter 4:10–11

For more on the Samaritan Woman, read John 4.

# The Samaritan Woman

## She owned her brokenness and accepted what Jesus had to offer.

The encounter must have seemed scandalous at first. A Jewish man—a Jewish teacher, no less—speaking kindly to a Samaritan woman? Asking her to draw water for him? Such things were just not done in Sychar.

Yet there was nothing sordid or untoward about the man's approach. He had no ulterior motive or hidden agenda. Stranger still, he showed no animosity or condescension toward her. He didn't call her names or make her feel less than human. A welcome change, no doubt.

Instead, the man talked about thirst—not a physical thirst, but a spiritual thirst. A thirst of the soul.

Something in his words must have reverberated deep inside her. She was no stranger to that thirst, that longing for something. Perhaps that's what had driven her to marry five different men and take up residence with a sixth, all to no avail. Those experiences only confirmed that her thirst couldn't be quenched by human love or fleeting relationships.

When Jesus offered water that would quench her thirst forever—a bubbling spring of eternal life—the Samaritan woman eagerly accepted. She didn't downplay her condition. She owned her brokenness and shame. She admitted that her soul was thirsty and that she needed what Jesus offered.

That was only the first thing she did right. The second was to share the news of the Messiah and his living water with others. She spread the word throughout the town. Thanks to her testimony, others came to see what Jesus was all about—and were also filled with his living water.

Every soul thirsts for Jesus and the eternal life he gives. Yet not everyone understands how to get it. That's where those of us who are familiar with the fountain come in. You may not feel comfortable in the role of a traditional "evangelist." That's fine. Instead, why not think of yourself simply as one thirsty person telling another thirsty person where to find water?

*Life Lesson: The testimony you have to share may be exactly what someone else needs to hear.*

## Jacob's Well

The well that serves as the backdrop for this story—Jacob's well (John 4:6)—is not mentioned anywhere else in the Bible. It still exists today near the ruins of ancient Shechem and is over 100 feet deep.

For more on the Woman Caught in Adultery, read John 8.

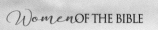

# The Woman Caught in Adultery

## She received mercy instead of the death sentence.

### It Takes Two

Where is the guilty man in this story? The Law of Moses demanded that both culprits of an adulterous crime be put to death (see Leviticus 20:10; Deut. 22:22–24). It appears the religious leaders whisked him off in order to use the woman alone to attempt to trap Jesus.

She must have been terrified. She'd been caught in the act of adultery and taken into custody by several of the religious leaders of Jerusalem—some men who weren't known for their tolerant or forgiving natures.

A small mob dragged her to the temple, where Jesus of Nazareth was teaching. Even in her panic, the woman must have sensed that the religious leaders were keen to prove their superiority to Jesus.

Her captors paraded her in front of the crowd that had gathered. "Teacher," they said to Jesus, "this woman was caught sleeping with a man who isn't her husband. The Law of Moses teaches that a woman like this should be stoned to death! What do you say?" (John 8:4–5).

That must have sent the woman's heart racing. Surely she realized her fate was out of her hands. She had no voice in these proceedings, no way to mount a defense or even beg for mercy. She was merely a pawn in some religious debate. Her captors were using her to try to trap Jesus with his own words.

Needless to say, she cared little about the finer points of their arguments. What mattered to her was the very real outcome that hung in the balance. She'd committed an offense that was punishable by death, according to the religious laws of Israel. And this mob was just zealous enough to start gathering stones.

Everything, it seemed, hinged on Jesus' response.

If the woman held her breath waiting for his answer, she probably turned a couple shades of blue. Jesus didn't reply to the accusations—not verbally, at least. Instead, he started writing something on the ground.

His opponents grew angry. Their questions became demands. The woman's pulse surely quickened again. How far were they prepared to go to provoke a response?

Just as the tension reached its breaking point, Jesus stood up and said, "If any of you have never sinned, then go ahead and throw the first stone at her!" (John 8:7). Then he went back to writing on the ground.

Her captors looked at each other, unsure what to do next. The elders among them shook their heads and walked away. One by one, the younger ones followed suit until only the woman and Jesus remained.

Then Jesus stood up again and said to the woman, "Where is everyone? Isn't there anyone left to accuse you?" (John 8:10).

"No, sir," she said (8:11a).

And Jesus said, "I am not going to accuse you either. You may go now, but don't sin anymore" (8:11b). There was a kindness in his voice, but no trace of playfulness. It was obvious he took her sin seriously.

Yet Jesus showed her mercy. He didn't want to see her punished; instead, he wanted her to experience what it is to be forgiven, to be clean, to have a fresh start.

Jesus wants the same for us too, no matter what we've done. If the woman caught in adultery could receive God's mercy, anyone can.

*Life Lesson:* **Nothing you've done is beyond God's ability to forgive.**

For more on Mary Magdalene, read John 20.

# Mary Magdalene

## She wholeheartedly served and followed Jesus.

Shortly after Jesus' arrest, most of his disciples—his brave, burly band of followers—scattered in terror to parts unknown. To be identified with Jesus of Nazareth was to risk a fate similar to his. Only a few people stayed with Jesus to the bitter end.

One of them was Mary Magdalene. Once upon a time, she'd been an outcast—and for good reason. Being possessed by seven demons does not exactly endear a person to her neighbors and acquaintances. But one word from Jesus had changed all that. The demons left her, and she became a new person.

Mary Magdalene also became a faithful follower of Jesus—perhaps the most devoted person in his entourage. She and a few other women traveled with Jesus and made sure he and his disciples were properly cared for. Though her work was rarely publicized, her contributions were vital to Jesus' ministry.

How devoted was she? After Jesus' resurrection, she discovered his empty tomb and talked to angels who were sitting inside it. She alerted the disciples. She was the first person to encounter the risen Lord.

Even among Jesus' most fervent followers, Mary stands apart. She seems to have understood better than anyone that a redeemed life becomes the property of the Redeemer.

Anyone looking to make a difference in this world through discipleship or ministry would be wise to take cues from Mary Magdalene. The woman had no use for half measures. She didn't compartmentalize her faith. She wholeheartedly gave of herself to serve Jesus.

*Life Lesson:* **The secret to being a difference-making disciple of Christ is to go all-in—to give him every part of your life.**

Detail of *Mary Kissing the Feet of the Crucified Jesus,* Italian, early 14th century

## Baseless Rumors

Over the centuries, many stories have spread concerning the identity of Mary Magdalene. Some people have falsely claimed she was a prostitute and the sinful woman described in Luke 7:37. Others have speculated she was Jesus' wife. Still others have sensationalized her by claiming she alone received special revelations from Jesus. None of these rumors are rooted in Scripture.

# THE NEW ERA WOMEN:

## Eight Women Who Served the Early Church through Evangelism and Discipleship

Jesus dealt a severe blow to gender bias during his earthly ministry. Not only was he an equal-opportunity teacher when it came to selecting his audience and staffing his entourage; he counted women among his closest friends.

Jesus opened the doors of his ministry to women, and they responded with a fervor and dedication that often put their male counterparts to shame. At his crucifixion, when Jesus needed his followers most, nearly all the sympathetic faces he saw in the crowd were female. Likewise, the very first disciples to discover his empty tomb and announce his resurrection were women.

It follows, then, that women would be given key leadership roles in the efforts at evangelism and discipleship that followed Jesus' return to heaven. The first-century church survived and thrived, thanks in large part to the contributions of Jesus' female followers. Engaged and empowered, these "new era" women helped spread Christ's message throughout the Roman Empire and beyond.

In this chapter, we'll look at eight women who seized the opportunity to transcend society's artificial limitations and make a difference for Christ's kingdom:

- Dorcas, whose death was mourned to such an extent that God used the apostle Peter to bring her back to life

- Mary, mother of John Mark, who welcomed Christians into her home even during the height of Jewish and Roman persecution

- Lydia, a successful businesswoman who helped shape Paul's ministry to Gentiles

- Bernice, the sister of Herod who recognized the truth in Paul's teaching and later risked her life to save God's people

- Priscilla, who served as a key ally to Paul and a mentor to Apollos

- Phoebe, who used her considerable personal and financial resources in service to God and his people

- Eunice, who was married to an unbeliever yet still managed to maintain a Christian household

- Lois, whose godly lifestyle and hunger for Christian teaching served as examples to her grandson Timothy

# Dorcas

She built a legacy of faith
and good works.

I f you want to know how people really feel about you, give dying a try. That's one thing we learn from the New Testament story of Dorcas (who was also known as Tabitha).

The scene at Dorcas's wake was bizarre, even by biblical standards. The reaction to her death went far beyond traditional grief. Her mourners simply could not come to grips with the hole left by her passing—not just in their own lives, but in the whole community, especially in the lives of the poor and needy.

The widows who were present carried Dorcas's handiwork, the garments she'd made for them, showing them to anyone who would look. Dorcas's love and concern for the women must have been evident in the quality of her work. Her friends and acquaintances seemed genuinely distraught that no one would be able to fill her shoes.

The fact that Dorcas made garments for widows suggests that she may have been a widow herself. In first-century Jewish culture, widows helped take care of those in need. If this was the case for Dorcas, she found a way to turn her loss into hope and encouragement for other women. And she did so with such a passion and loving spirit that, when she died, no one could take her place.

That prospect was too much to bear for those to whom she had ministered. Those attending her wake weren't so much mourning her loss as they were asking for an encore of her life.

God heard their cries. Not coincidentally, the apostle Peter was nearby, so two of the mourners were dispatched to fetch him. When Peter arrived, he cleared the room. He then prayed over Dorcas's body and told her to get up. Ever the servant, Dorcas did as she was asked.

## The Town of Joppa

Joppa, a Judean seaport located about 38 miles from Jerusalem, is no insignificant town in the biblical narrative. It was from Joppa that the prophet Jonah attempted to escape God by boarding a ship set sail for Spain (see Jonah 1). Through the life, death, and raising to life of Dorcas, many people in Joppa believed in Jesus (see Acts 9:42). While in Joppa, Peter received the divine vision that finally convinced him that God extends the invitation to his kingdom to non-Jews as well as to Jews (see Acts 11).

She lived to serve another day—and many more days after that.

Oh, to have a wake like the one for Dorcas! To have people mourn your loss—not just because of their personal grief but also because of the impact of your service to God and your community. Oh, to make such a difference in other people's lives!

The question we must ask is this: What can we do—today, tomorrow, and every day—to build such a legacy? In other words, how can we impact people's lives in ways that truly make a difference?

*Life Lesson:* **Every day you have an opportunity to build a God-honoring legacy that will extend far beyond your circle of acquaintances.**

For more on Dorcas, read Acts 9.

For more on Mary, mother of John Mark, read Acts 12.

Sweet Home

# Mary, Mother of John Mark

## She made her home and her heart available for God's use.

Persecution was a fact of life for Christians from the earliest days of Jesus' ministry. To be a follower of Christ was to be an enemy of the powerful Jewish religious establishment—and later the even more powerful Roman Empire. If you found yourself on the wrong side of either group, you would suffer the consequences.

As the church grew after Jesus' return to heaven, the persecution intensified. King Herod Agrippa executed the apostle James and arrested the apostle Peter. While scores of believers fell away or went into hiding in fear for their safety, one household in Jerusalem remained steadfast in its support of Jesus' ministry. One house welcomed believers of all stripes, at all times. So when Peter escaped from prison, there was one logical place for him to go.

The house belonged to a woman named Mary. Needless to say, opening her house to the leaders and rank and file of the fledgling church placed her at great risk. And this was a woman who had a lot to lose. For one thing, she had a son named John Mark (the same John Mark who prompted the split between Paul and Barnabas; see Acts 15:36–41). In addition, the fact that Mary had servants in her household suggests that her family was wealthy. And with wealth came social standing.

Yet Mary risked it all to show hospitality to those in need. She created a home where believers felt welcomed and safe. In the process, she set an example for all Christians.

The more welcoming we are to those in need, to people with nowhere else to go—especially God's people—the more useful we are to the Lord. When we make our homes and our lives available to God, he will do amazing things in and through us.

How many lives were saved as a result of Mary's hospitality? How many lives will be changed as a result of yours?

*Life Lesson:* **The more hospitable you are to those in need, the better view you'll have of God's awesome work.**

## Practice Hospitality

God's Word commands and encourages us to joyfully show hospitality to friends and strangers alike.

- "Take care of God's needy people and welcome strangers into your home." (Romans 12:13)
- "Be sure to welcome strangers into your home. By doing this, some people have welcomed angels as guests, without even knowing it." (Hebrews 13:2)
- "Welcome people into your home and don't grumble about it." (1 Peter 4:9)

BE SINCERE IN YOUR LOVE FOR OTHERS. HATE
EVERYTHING THAT IS EVIL AND HOLD TIGHT
TO EVERYTHING THAT IS GOOD. LOVE EACH
OTHER AS BROTHERS AND SISTERS AND HONOR
OTHERS MORE THAN YOU DO YOURSELF.

**ROMANS 12:9-13**

NEVER GIVE UP. EAGERLY FOLLOW THE HOLY SPIRIT AND SERVE THE LORD. LET YOUR HOPE MAKE YOU GLAD. BE PATIENT IN TIME OF TROUBLE AND NEVER STOP PRAYING. TAKE CARE OF GOD'S NEEDY PEOPLE AND WELCOME STRANGERS INTO YOUR HOME.

For more on Lydia, read Acts 16.

# Lydia

## Her vibrant personality shaped her ministry.

Lydia likely had a classic type-A personality. A successful businesswoman, she dealt in expensive purple cloth. Her clients were the movers and shakers of first-century society. She was comfortable in their midst, whether they were Gentiles like her or Jews.

After a conversation with the apostle Paul, Lydia gave her life to Christ—something very few Gentiles had done up to that point. Even more unusual was the fact that Lydia didn't convert to Judaism first. Apparently she was less concerned about how things had been done in the past than how things could be done from that moment on. She preferred to set the curve rather than follow it.

Lydia's first order of business after she and her family were baptized was to extend an offer of hospitality to Paul and his companions. There was more to the offer than met the eye, though. It represented a test of Paul's commitment to the Gentiles. Paul's presence in Lydia's home would go a long way toward legitimizing Christian ministry to non-Jews.

Paul accepted Lydia's invitation. He and his companions stayed in her home.

Every believer can learn from Lydia's example. She allowed her personality to shape her ministry. She thought big and seized opportunities as they presented themselves to her. She risked rejection as she took her first steps in serving the Lord (Paul very well could have said no and dealt a blow to her social standing).

*Life Lesson: If you're willing to allow your personality to shape your ministry, seize opportunities as they arise, and take risks for the sake of serving God, then you can be a difference maker in your Christian walk.*

### The Westward Spread of the Gospel

Paul's journey from Troas to Philippi marks the passage of the gospel from Asia to Europe (see Acts 16). When Lydia gave her life to Christ in Philippi (Greece), she became the first Gentile to convert to Christianity in the Western world and immediately led her household in being baptized. Since households were the basic social unit of the early church, Lydia was in effect the leader of a local church.

For more on Bernice, read Acts 25–26.

# Bernice

## She heard the truth of the gospel.

Bernice and her brother, King Agrippa, were in Jerusalem to pay their respects to Festus, the newly appointed governor of Judea, when they were offered an intriguing opportunity. It seems Festus had inherited a vexing judicial matter from his predecessor. The Jewish religious leaders had accused the apostle Paul of blasphemy and demanded that he be put to death. Their accusations hinged on the fact that Paul claimed a crucified man named Jesus had come back to life—an outrageous assertion, to be sure, but hardly a capital offense. The problem was that Festus had no idea how to go about investigating such a matter. And the Jewish officials were quite insistent.

Bernice and Agrippa, both of whom were Jewish by birth, asked to speak to Paul. No strangers to the Jewish Scriptures, they wanted to know how he could justify his claim.

Seizing the opportunity, Paul made a masterful presentation of the gospel disguised as a legal defense. He used the words of the Hebrew prophets to show Bernice and Agrippa that Jesus was everything the Jewish people had been waiting for. Paul even shared his own encounter with the risen Christ as proof of the resurrection.

Paul pointedly asked Agrippa (and Bernice, by extension) if he believed in the prophets. The apostle was asking the king to make a commitment to Christ, and Agrippa knew it. Agrippa asked, "In such a short time do you think you can talk me into being a Christian?" (Acts 26:28).

Agrippa's words revealed his mind-set. The king didn't reject Paul's claims outright, which may suggest that something resonated with him—something he wanted to give some more thought to. He was almost persuaded, but he needed time to formulate his response.

Bernice remained silent through it all. Could it be that Paul's words had a similar impact on her? Did she too wrestle with her response to the gospel?

History offers a tantalizing postscript to the story. Years later, in AD 66, Bernice risked her life to save Jews who were being massacred by the Roman leader Gessius Florus. In fact, she was almost killed by Roman soldiers, and her palace was burned down in the ensuing war.

Could it be that a devotion to Christ inspired her sacrifice?

No one knows for sure. But Bernice serves as a reminder of those today who are almost persuaded that Jesus is who he claims to be—people who are mostly convinced that he can make a difference in their lives, who are on the fence about making a commitment to him.

What do they need from us? How can we help them make up their minds? The more thought we give to these questions, the better chance we have of being used by God to help them.

*Life Lesson:* **The way you live your Christian faith may be the catalyst that moves someone from "almost persuaded" to "persuaded."**

## All in the Family

Bernice and her two sons—Berenicianus
and Hyrcanus—lived with her older brother
Agrippa II after her first husband (Herod of Chalcis,
who was also her uncle) died.

## House Church

First Corinthians 16:19 reveals that Priscilla and Aquila opened up their home in Ephesus to serve as a church.

For more on Priscilla, read Acts 18; Romans 16:3–5.

# Priscilla

## Her support and encouragement helped build the early church.

Every would-be disciple needs a friend like Priscilla. The leaders of the first-century church, including Paul, Barnabas, and Apollos, were able to do what they did because they had the support and assistance of Priscilla and others like her.

The Bible doesn't say how Priscilla became a Christian, but it's clear she was one of the first converts in Rome. She and her husband, Aquila, relocated to Corinth after Emperor Claudius expelled all Jews from the capital city.

Priscilla and Aquila were tent makers by profession, as was the apostle Paul. That may explain why he made a point of visiting them when he traveled to Corinth. Paul ended up staying and working with the couple for an extended time. When he finally set sail for Syria, he took Priscilla and Aquila with him.

Along the way, the three of them decided that Priscilla's and Aquila's ministry gifts were most needed in the city of Ephesus. The couple may have been instrumental in planting or nurturing the church there. It was in Ephesus that they encountered Apollos, who boldly proclaimed the message of Jesus in the synagogue. Priscilla and her husband noticed that Apollos' knowledge of certain Christian doctrines (including baptism) was limited, so they took him home to explain the way of God more fully. They helped prepare the rookie evangelist for the ministry that lay ahead.

Paul's shout-out to the couple in Romans 16:3–4 is especially telling: "Give my greetings to Priscilla and Aquila. They have not only served Christ Jesus together with me, but they have even risked their lives for me. I am grateful to them and so are all the Gentile churches."

Priscilla was so instrumental in church ministry that the usual customs concerning women of the first century seem to have been suspended for her. Traditionally, when spouses are mentioned together in Scripture, the husband is named first. However, in more than half of the passages in which Priscilla and Aquila are mentioned, Priscilla is introduced first.

Likewise, women were generally prohibited from teaching others. Yet Priscilla was obviously a teacher. Some Bible scholars have even gone so far as to suggest that Priscilla is the anonymous writer of the book of Hebrews.

The manner in which Priscilla built her reputation serves as an example to us all. She didn't set out to break down barriers or wave banners. She didn't draw attention to herself. She simply used the talents and abilities God had given her for his service. Her leadership style was such that she didn't care who got the recognition; she just wanted to make sure they were well equipped for the role they would play.

*Life Lesson: **Providing comfort, direction, and encouragement to people in ministry is itself a vital ministry.***

For more on Phoebe, read Romans 16.

# Phoebe

## She gave so that others could grow.

The apostle Paul closed his letter to the Romans with some heartfelt personal commendations and greetings. The first person on his list is a woman who apparently was unknown to the believers in Rome:

*I have good things to say about Phoebe, who is a leader in the church at Cenchreae. Welcome her in a way that is proper for someone who has faith in the Lord and is one of God's own people. Help her in any way you can. After all, she has proved to be a respected leader for many others, including me.* (Romans 16:1–2)

Phoebe's importance to Paul's ministry is evident in the likelihood that the apostle entrusted her to deliver his letter to the Romans. She served as a deacon in her church, which suggests she was known for her integrity, leadership, and spiritual maturity. Put simply, Phoebe was committed to helping others. As far as Paul was concerned, she was worthy of honor because she was a servant of Christ Jesus.

We can find two sources of inspiration from Phoebe's commendation in Romans 16. The first, of course, is Phoebe herself. Paul brought her to the Romans' attention for good reason. Here was a woman the new believers could model themselves after.

The phrase "To whom much is given much is expected" may sound cautionary to some, but Phoebe seems to have embraced it as a challenge. Her material wealth wasn't an end unto itself; it was a tool for ministry, as were her personal gifts and abilities. God used her in a powerful way because she used her resources to honor him.

Phoebe seems to have mastered the art of servanthood. If the same can be said of us at the end of our lives, we will count ourselves among the truly blessed.

The second source of inspiration in Phoebe's story comes from the apostle Paul. He wanted to make sure this faithful woman's contributions to the Christian cause did not go unnoticed. He drew attention to her work and held her up as an example of Christian service.

In so doing, he set an example for the rest of us. Do you know someone like Phoebe—a faithful servant who's content to use their gifts in anonymity? What can you do to help show this person that his or her ministry is appreciated and that it's making a difference in people's lives?

*Life Lesson:* **Even a small act of God-honoring service can have a tremendous impact on someone else.**

## True to Her Name

The apostle Paul held out Phoebe's shining example of servanthood as a beacon for the early church (and us) to follow. Interestingly enough, the name *Phoebe* comes from the Greek word *Phoebus*, which means "bright and shining."

### Eunice's Hometown

Eunice most likely raised Timothy in the town of Lystra, a Roman colony with no synagogue. Today the town exists as Klistra, in the country of Turkey.

# Eunice

## She left a legacy of faithfulness for her son.

Eunice was the mother of Timothy. That's the shorthand version of her biblical biography—one that likely would have satisfied her. Her son was, after all, a pivotal figure in the first-century church.

However, when the facts are examined in a nonpatriarchal light, one could make a strong case for reversing those identifiers: Timothy was the son of Eunice.

This remarkable woman served as a spiritual role model to her child. She instructed him in the ways of a faith that very few people understood at that time. The fact that she grasped the nuances of Jesus' new covenant and was able to share them with her son qualified her as a teacher on par with any of the heavyweights of the faith—including the apostle Paul.

The fact that she did so with only her mother, Lois, to help qualifies Eunice as something even more remarkable. Nowhere in Scripture is Timothy's father mentioned in connection with his son's spiritual development. As a Gentile nonbeliever, he left that responsibility to his devout Jewish wife and her equally devout mother.

Paul refers to Eunice in glowing terms in 2 Timothy 1:5. It is likely that she was able to maintain her relationship with her unbelieving husband while at the same time minimizing his influence on their son's Christian walk. She had to create a spiritually nurturing environment in her home without ostracizing her husband. Any Christian who's married to a nonbeliever knows the delicate balance that's required to pull off such a feat.

Eunice's example is an inspiration to all of us. She took seriously her responsibility to be a godly spouse who honored her partner—as well as a godly parent who instilled a love for God and his Word in her child.

*Life Lesson: **If you take seriously your responsibility to raise God-honoring, spiritually mature children, God will bless your efforts and make sure you have the resources and support you need.***

For more on Eunice,
read Acts 16:1; 2 Timothy 1.

Memorize these laws and think about them . . . Teach them to your children. Talk about them all the time—whether you're at home or walking along the road or going to bed at night, or getting up in the morning.

*Deuteronomy 11:18–19*

For more on Lois,
read 2 Timothy 1.

# Lois

## She helped to mold Timothy into a spiritual leader.

Sir Isaac Newton paid tribute to his scientific forerunners when he said, "If I have seen a little further, it is by standing on the shoulders of giants." The same principle applies to faith. Timothy, the young pastor who became a protégé of the apostle Paul, could attest to that. In his case, the giants were in his own home.

The first was his mother, Eunice (see pages 186–187). The second was his grandmother Lois. These two women passed on their deep and abiding Christian faith to him. They molded him into a spiritual leader.

Was that Lois's intent all along—to send her grandson into the world with a knowledge of Scripture and a faith that would change lives? Did she dream of his becoming an influential pastor or evangelist one day? Her motivation isn't clear in the biblical narrative. What is clear is the influence she had on her grandson.

Timothy was able to make a difference in other people's lives because his grandmother had cared enough to make a difference in his. Her godly example shaped him in ways he may not even have realized.

Lois's work in Timothy's life inspires each of us to think of our own faith in generational terms. Looking backward, we may ask ourselves, *Who inspired me? Who taught me about God's Word? Who showed me what it means to be a Christian? Who helped me recognize what a servant looks like?* More to the point: *What can I learn from their example?*

Looking forward, we may ask, *Who might benefit from my spiritual knowledge and experience? Whom can I mentor in the Christian faith? Whom can I prepare for Christian service?*

Not every training opportunity is formal, of course. Some of the most helpful instruction or inspiration can take place through casual conversation or simply by hanging out with someone. The key is to prayerfully prepare for such opportunities and to seize them when they arise. Don't underestimate the life-changing potential of a single piece of advice or word of encouragement.

*Life Lesson:* **Every interaction you have with someone of a younger generation is an opportunity for spiritual instruction, inspiration, or encouragement.**

### Wisdom for Grandparents

King David recognized the vital role that grandparents and older adults have in passing the torch of faith to younger generations: "You are wonderful, LORD, and you deserve all praise, because you are much greater than anyone can understand. Each generation will announce to the next your wonderful and powerful deeds" (Psalm 145:3–4).

# History and Mission of American Bible Society

Established in 1816, American Bible Society's history is closely intertwined with the history of a nation whose founding preceded its own by less than a generation. In fact, the Society's early leadership reads like a Who's Who of patriots and other notable Americans of the time. Its first president was Elias Boudinot, formerly the President of the Continental Congress. John Jay, John Quincy Adams, DeWitt Clinton, and chronicler of the new nation James Fennimore Cooper also played significant roles, as would Rutherford B. Hayes and Benjamin Harrison in later generations.

From the beginning, the Bible Society's mission was to respond to the civic and spiritual needs of a fast-growing, diverse population in a rapidly expanding nation. From the new frontier beyond the Appalachian Mountains, missionaries sent back dire reports of towns that did not have a single copy of the Bible to share among its citizens. State and local Bible Societies did not have the resources, network, or capability of filling this growing need. Only a national organization would be able to do so. Once founded, ABS committed itself to organizational and technological innovation. No longer subject to British restrictions, ABS could set up its own printing plants, develop better qualities of paper and ink, and establish a network of colporteurs to get the Bibles to the people who needed them.

Reaching out to diverse audiences has always been at the heart of ABS's mission. Scriptures were made available to Native American peoples in their own languages—in Delaware in 1818, followed soon by Mohawk, Seneca, Ojibwa, Cherokee, and others. French and Spanish Bibles were published for the Louisiana Territory, Florida, and the Southwest. By the 1890s ABS was printing or distributing Scriptures in German, Portuguese, Chinese, Italian, Russian, Danish, Polish, Hungarian, Czech, and other languages to meet the spiritual needs of an increasing immigrant population. In 1836, seventy-five years before the first Braille Bibles were produced, ABS was providing Scriptures to the blind in "raised letter" editions. Responding to the need for Bibles in the languages and formats that speak most deeply to people's hearts continues to be a priority of ABS. Through its partnerships with other national Bible Societies, ABS can provide some portion of Scripture in almost any language that has a written form. It has also been able to provide Braille Scriptures for the blind; recorded Scriptures for the visually impaired, dyslexic, and people who have not yet learned to read; as well as Bible stories in sign language for the deaf.

The Bible Society's founders and their successors have always understood the Bible as a text that can speak to people's deepest needs during times of crisis. ABS distributed its first Scriptures to the military in 1817 when it provided New Testaments to the crew of the USS *John Adams,* a frigate that had served in the War of 1812 and was continuing its service to the country by protecting the American Coast from pirates. During the Civil War, ABS provided Testaments to both northern and southern forces, and has continued to provide Bibles and Testaments to the U.S. military forces during every subsequent war, conflict, and operation. During the painful post-Reconstruction era when Jim Crow laws prevailed in many parts of the nation, ABS was able to provide Scriptures to African Americans through its partnership with the Agency Among Colored People of the South and through the historic Black churches. This faith that the Word of God speaks in special ways during times of crisis continues to inform ABS's mission. In recent years the Bible Society has produced Scripture booklets addressing the needs of people with HIV and AIDS and for those experiencing profound loss due to acts of terrorism and natural disasters.

Translation and scholarship are key components to the Bible Society's mission of faithfully and powerfully communicating the Word of God. In the mid-twentieth century, ABS, in partnership with the United Bible Societies, developed innovative theories and practices of translation, under the leadership of Eugene A. Nida. First, they insisted that all of the Bible translations they sponsored be done exclusively by native speakers, with biblical and linguistic experts serving only as translation consultants to provide technical support and guidance. From the lively and heart-felt translations that resulted, Bible Society scholars were able to see the power of translations that were rendered not on a word-for-word basis, but on a meaning-for-meaning basis that respected the natural rhythms and idioms of the target languages. This practice of "functional equivalence" translation led to a new line of Bible translations in English and was, in part, responsible for the explosion of new translations of the Bible that came out in the past thirty years. These include the Bible Society's own *Good News Translation* and *Contemporary English Version,* as well as other non-English translations.

As an organization dedicated to preparing well-researched, faithful translations, ABS has necessarily committed itself to the pursuit of scholarly excellence. In cooperation with the United Bible Societies, ABS has helped develop and publish authoritative Greek and Hebrew texts, Handbooks on the different books of the Bible, dictionaries, and other technical aids. To provide the most up-to-date training and the broadest access to all the relevant disciplines, the Nida Institute for Biblical Scholarship offers professional development seminars and workshops, hosts symposia, and publishes a journal and monograph series, all in an effort to ensure that translators communicate the Word of God powerfully to God's people around the world. For churches and readers seeking a deeper understanding of the Bible and its background, ABS has developed study Bibles, multimedia video translations with DVD extras, Scriptures in special formats, and website resources.

For almost two centuries, ABS has maintained its commitment to innovation and excellence. While the challenges it has faced over the years have changed, the Society's mission has remained constant—*to make the Bible available to every person in a language and format each can understand and afford so all people may experience its life-changing message.*

To find out more about American Bible Society please go to www.americanbible.org or www.bibles.com.